The

The Plan

A Guide for Women
Raising African American Boys
From Conception to College

LAWSON BUSH V, EDWARD C. BUSH,
KENNON MITCHELL,
A. MAJADI AND SALIM FARAJI

THIRD WORLD PRESS

Progressive Black Publishing Since 1967

Chicago

Third World Press
Publishers since 1967
Chicago

First Edition
Printed in the United States of America

Library of Congress Control Number: 2011943078

ISBN 13: 978-0-88378-328-3

18 17 16 15 14 13 12   8 7 6 5 4 3 2 1

Cover and Layout by Relana Johnson

W e dedicate our book to those scholar/activists such as Haki Madhubuti, Na'im Akbar, Jawanza Kunjufu, and Jewelle Taylor Gibbs, who in the 1980s and early 1990s raised our consciousness concerning African men and boys in the United States.

As educators, we must speak directly to our beloved Ancestor Asa Hilliard III. Most of us literally carried your books around with us in our college backpacks. Your work gave us the courage and the knowledge to challenge our professors and others. More importantly, your work gave us the foundation to build programs for our boys (and girls) and the trajectory to produce additional scholarship in your tradition of telling our uncompromised truth. For this, on the behalf of African peoples worldwide, we thank you and we love you!

Acknowledgements

We thank Sister Dr. Tonia (Amma) Causey-Bush for being the internal editor of our project. Also we are grateful to our colleagues/sisters/mothers who provided us with important feedback on our manuscript. Lastly, we thank Baba Dr. Molefi Kete Asante for his advice during the publishing process, writing the foreword, and for being a paragon scholar/warrior/elder.

Contents

Foreword

Five black men have written a compelling book on raising boys from conception through college. Lawson Bush, V, Edward Bush, Kennon Mitchell, A. Majadi, and Salim Faraji have contributed their theoretical, analytical, and experiential skills to this monumental endeavor. One thing that strikes me is their enthusiasm about *The Plan*. They have arrived at this energetic place in the discourse on raising black boys from different perspectives yet they have converged at the same place. Black mothers are responsible for the vast majority of education, training, personal skills, ethical development, and discipline of young black boys in the American society. Of course, the authors of *The Plan* know precisely the arguments that have been given to explain this situation. They are conscious of the racism, segregation, brutality, and discrimination that have conspired to create the social maladies in the African American community. Beyond the point of their concern however, is the fact that they have studied the social and psychological condition of black boys and men in order to understand the best program for healing the wounded spirits, directing the frequently misguided, and providing mothers with an informed perspective on how to cope and succeed with boys who are without present fathers.

The Plan does not fill in all of the blanks but it does provide the reader with substantive thinking that will surely impact the mothers who read it. However, the book is not merely for women; it is for all of those who work with and train black boys. *The Plan* is not a Holy Bible or Koran but it is something more specific: it is a distilled account of and narrative for the raising of African American boys by their mothers. The authoritative ring of *The Plan* strikes me because the book speaks to the common concerns, ordinary inquiries, and special needs of mothers who have inherited the task of raising black boys.

There is no doubt that the vicissitudes of living in

America have often damaged the relationship between mothers and their sons. While the great majority of mothers raise their sons with little or no difficulty, we know that there are large numbers of mothers who are struggling to manage their sons. The absentee father is a cornerstone of this situation but there is no guarantee that the presence of the father would create a better opportunity for the black boy. In some cases, the father and the son are at odds with each other and the mother has to intercede. Nevertheless, most research and experience suggest that the presence of the father is a positive factor in the developmental growth of most boys. Yet the fact that more than fifty percent of young black boys are being raised by their mothers suggests that men have been opting out of the fatherhood role. Mothers usually cannot opt out of the motherhood role and therefore are often left as the only adult in a household with the children.

The Plan seeks to answer the questions that are most often asked by mothers trying to raise black boys. One question they put to rest very early is whether or not a woman can raise a boy? The answer, of course, is yes she can if she uses the guidelines established in the Plan.

This book is built along the foundations that are most consistent with the African culture. This is why the authors chose to return to the sources of the best ethical and moral ideas of the African culture. Kemet, the classical culture most ancient and documented, is the repository of many ideas and concepts and the authors have not forgotten the contributions of the ancient thinkers.

I see this project as one of the main reconstructive tasks of the African intellectual. We must reconnect our people and our communities to the essential characteristics of the best of our traditions. If we cannot create a renaissance, a resurgence in our own cultural forms and practices related to our values, we will forever have children who are lost and incapable of becoming all they can be. This is why The Plan seeks to address the problem of mothers raising black boys. It is the objective of the powerful prescription found in this book to elevate not only the discourse around raising black boys but also the practice itself.

Of course, if every black father would simply engage

their sons the tasks of the mothers would be infinitely easier. Nothing can take the place of the twin roles and responsibilities of a mother and a father. However, since we are at a crisis point in our contemporary history, which may continue into the foreseeable future, it is essential that mothers understand as much as they can about the nature of the process of bringing black boys to maturity without disaster.

Ironically there was a time when mothers and fathers understood how to establish environments for the protection and safety of their children even in a racist society. We were taught the nature of anti-Africanism and shown the results of not being able to function intelligently within the social context created by notions of white racial domination.

Alas, what we are told by the authors of *The Plan* is that all is not lost and that the use of cultural grounding to center young black males is not only possible, but also necessary. Centering children in their culture and history, as has been demonstrated by experience, is the key to rejuvenating the education of male and female children. The fact that these brothers-authors have concentrated on black mothers raising black boys speaks to the fact that we are in an emergency mode with the exploding social and cultural chaos around young brothers. In the end, we shall gain the victory over the devastation caused by dislocation and *The Plan* will prove to be a major part of the campaign for social and cultural sanity.

Molefi Kete Asante
Author, *An Afrocentric Manifesto*

Introduction

How should you prepare to have a son? Does the food you eat, music you listen to, and people you hang around affect your son while you are pregnant? Is your son's name important? Can a single mother raise a boy into a man? What does our history tell us about Black mother/son relationships? Do you really need a parenting plan? Should your son fear you? Should you spank your son? Should you allow your son to cry? Should you allow your son to grow long hair or to have an earring (or earrings)? What should you expect from the public school system? How do you approach school so that your son gets what he needs? What should you teach your son about sexuality, romance, and love? What is a rite-of-passage? How do you know if you are doing a good job? How do you monitor your son's progress toward college? What can you expect of your son while he is in college? Who do you want your son to be?

Above is just a sampling of the many critical questions that we provide direct answers to and/or provide the space and direction to develop a planned approach to answer on your own. This book is specifically geared toward mothers—both married and singled—of Black boys. We want to provide tools for parents of all boys including those who have had their share of challenges in school, those who may have had encounters with the juvenile justice system and those who appear to be on the right track. In each case when concerning Black males, we, as advocates for youth, and you as the mother can never let our guard down and must be in a constant state of vigilance, planning, and action.

Thus the book, *The Plan*, and accompanying workbook could help you plan a path for your son. Both books are written and designed with the intention that they could be utilized throughout the developmental stages of your son's life, that is, from the prenatal stage through college. You will need a workbook for each son that you have in your household. It should have a highly visible and constant presence in their lives. In other words, be clear with your son that you have *The*

Plan for raising and preparing him.

Tell him that your parenting will not be perfect; however, it is intentional. To know that you have a plan will inspire your son. It will set a high level of clear expectations which will become embedded in his psyche and will in turn influence his behavior.

There has been extensive conversation about a woman's ability to raise sons to become men; and we will indeed weigh in on that dialogue in chapter I. Nevertheless, irrespective of whatever one's position is on your ability, there remains one significant fact: Black mothers, married or single, play an enormous role, perhaps you are even the most significant factor given the amount of time you spend with your sons in proportion to others, in raising boys to become men.

In Chapter II, we focus on the historical relationship between Black mothers and sons. African civilizations viewed this relationship as so sacred that it was distinguished as the key kinship bond for the anchoring and stabilizing of Black societies. We will illustrate through an examination of the founding of two African empires that the mother-son relationship served as the basis by which the independence and sovereignty of the society was established and defended.

We begin Chapter III dealing with the early development of a fetus and the potential impact diet, mood, sound, and the like may have on your developing son. We also introduce an exercise that will help you develop a parenting philosophy. Last, we discuss the importance and spiritual significance of a name and baby dedication/naming ceremony.

Ages one to four are critical with respect to your son's development and are the focus of Chapter IV. It is in this chapter where we engage such fundamental questions as: *Should your son fear you? Should you spank your son? Should you allow your son to play sports? Should you allow your son to grow long hair or to have an earring (or earrings)?* We also introduce the Manhood Development Progress Indicator (MDPI) which is a comprehensive planning tool designed to help you monitor the development of your son across areas such as Spirituality, African History and Culture, Love, and Survival/Protection over time or ages.

In Chapter V, we outline exactly what to expect from public schools, and more importantly, how to get what you need for your son out of them. We also talk about the importance of providing supplemental educational programs, chiefly a rite of passage. We provide, in the workbook, complete guidelines for conducting a family rite of passage.

In Chapter VI, we focus on adolescence and sexual development. We specifically describe why and how mothers must play an intricate role during this time period. We outline rules for dating and discuss abstinence, teen pregnancy, contraceptives, and STDs. Also, we provide worksheets in the workbook to track your son's progress towards college.

In the last chapter on college, we stress that your work is not over: As a matter of fact in many respects this is just the beginning. We provide the guidance to help you with financial aid, grades, homesickness, and social relationships all of which are topics you should be in dialogue with your son about as you help him successfully transition to the next phase of life.

We drew heavily upon our history, culture, and spirituality as African peoples to provide the foundation and context for *The Plan*. Additionally, the book and workbook were born out of over fifteen years of working directly with Black boys and their mothers as ministers, school teachers and administrators, directors and founders of manhood development, mentorship, Saturday school, after school, and rites-of-passages programs, researchers, and fathers. In terms of style, our prescriptions and recommendations are fairly straightforward. Thus, to remind the reader that we are dealing with real people and real situations, each chapter begins with a brief narrative of an actual event that came from our interactions, practices, or interviews with mothers with the exception of chapter II, which already provides you with stories about Black mothers and sons from antiquity to present.

The Plan

Chapter I

Beyond the Debate

Black Mothers Raising Our Sons

A Personal Story

Ms. Coles, a fifty-five year-old woman who was a single mother for most of her two boys' lives, spoke in great detail in an interview about how she had successfully raised her two sons. John was twenty-two and finishing up college and Mike, thirty-two, was a married father (a "great father" she added) of three children who was doing well in the business field. Ms. Coles spent over an hour sharing many wonderful stories of how she taught her sons how to deal with bullies, girls, school, and sex. Toward the end of the interview she was asked, "Can a woman teach her son how to be a man?" "Oh no honey!" she replied. She was then asked, "How did your sons become the men they are?" Ms. Coles sat in silence for a few minutes as tears began to fall down her face and then she spoke: "I guess I have been feeling so guilty because their father was not around thinking that I did not give them enough; but, my boys are fine—they are good men. It was hard but I did it."

There have been extensive conversations about Black mothers' ability to raise their sons to become men. Nevertheless, irrespective of whatever one's position is on their ability, there remains one significant fact: Black mothers, married or single, play an enormous role in the nurturing and development of both their sons and daughters. Perhaps they are even the most significant factor given the amount of time they spend with their sons in proportion to others, in raising boys to become men. Hence, their important place in childrearing underscores the notion that "a people will go as far as their women will take them."

Getting right to the heart of the matter: "Can Black Mothers Raise Our Sons?" Many people have much to say concerning the topic, yet, there has been very little research on the issue.[1] In fact, one of the authors of this book is one of the few scholars in the nation who has actually studied the relationship between Black mothers and sons. The two most popular statements when it comes to Black mothers raising boys are: "Woman can do many things for her son but when it is time for him to become a man, only another man can show him;" and "Black women raise their daughters and love their sons."

We have challenged first ourselves, then scholars, and Black men and women in general across the nation to show us the one thing that Black mothers could not teach their sons, that only men can—we have yet to find it. In all aspects of manhood development including self defense, how to dress, responsibility, spirituality, sexuality, health, finances, toughness, love, discipline, and more; we have found countless examples where Black mothers have successfully taught their sons these important aspects of manhood. Nevertheless, we are not saying that the one or perhaps few things that women cannot teach boys do not exist, but the fact that we are so hard pressed to find it or them is telling.

The important point here is not that we agree or disagree on whether there are some things that a woman cannot teach a man, rather, it is more important that we recognize and understand the vast areas of manhood that Black mothers do in fact impart and develop in their sons. We have provided you with a diagram from *Can Black Mothers Raise Our Sons?* to help illustrate this crucial point. (See Figure 1)

The region where the two spheres intersect represents the areas in males' lives that both mothers (women) and fathers (men) can potentially cultivate manhood: This represents a majority of what a boy needs to know, possess, and/or master in order to reach manhood. The gray region, where there is no overlap, represents the aspects of manhood that possibly only fathers (men) can teach. If there are aspects of manhood that only a man can teach then there may be aspects of manhood that only mothers (women) can teach a boy—the white area indicates this concept.

Additionally, we have added a second diagram to speak

to aspects of manhood that possibly neither mothers nor fathers can teach. (See Figure 2) This is represented as the white bottom region where there is no overlap. Possibly there are aspects of manhood only a third party can teach. We are speaking to the transformative spiritual energy of a community or a couple of people coming together for a purpose: to create, change, build, free, or, in this case, raise a boy into a man.

Do some Black mothers raise their daughters and love their sons? Yes. Do some Black fathers raise their daughters, and under the mantra "boys will be boys," only love their boys rather than raise them? Yes. Both are equally problematic yet most proclaimed advocates of Black males only blame mothers for this practice. Moreover, this irresponsible statement—only a Black man can show a boy how to become a man—contributes to the phenomena of some Black mothers only loving their sons rather than raising them. Some Black women relinquish or excuse themselves of the responsibility of raising their sons to become men because they have been brainwashed into believing that it is a man's job to do it. Thus, some women wait for a man that may or may not show while they possess much of what it takes to raise a man. We aim to put an end to this phenomenon, as we want you to be clear that your son cannot be raised into a man without you.

It is important that we clarify some of the issues and misconceptions surrounding single Black mothers as well.[2] Let us say right up front that we do not advocate single Black mothers raising boys alone. However, nor do we advocate two parents, man and woman, raising a boy alone, that is, without the support of an extended family network. Both situations may be risky to the development of Black boys.[3]

We cannot group all single Black mothers together; they are not the same. The single mother who is forty years old with a career who chose to be a single mother is different from the fifteen-year-old girl "that got pregnant." The public treats them the same when we blame them for the ills facing Black communities. Moreover, researchers have made the same mistake.[4] Scholars have suggested that single Black mothers are the cause of high school dropout and imprisonment rates among Black males but they do not take into account other factors that impact families.

For example, a boy lives with his mother and father until he is twelve years old. At age twelve, his parents after years of bitter fighting get a divorce and he now lives with only his mother. Two years later he commits a crime, goes to jail, and it is recorded that he is from a single-parent household. Scholars and others then erroneously come along to suggest that the boy's involvement with the penal system is because he is from a single-mother household. But in this example, it is more reasonable to assume that the boy having witnessed years of volatility in the home is the major source of what has caused him to be in trouble rather than him being a product of a single-family home.

Surely the number of Black female-headed households is of great concern particularly given that in some inner-city communities, upwards of 70 percent of Black boys are raised in single-parent homes. Nevertheless, we hope that we as a community will think more critically before we rush to blame Black mothers for the challenging conditions facing a significant number of Black boys today.

The growing epidemic of Black single mothers is symptomatic of larger issues facing our communities. We cannot underestimate the impact of being stripped of our culture. When you separate a people from their culture it is like separating a baby from his mother and expecting him to raise himself. The vestiges of African culture that were maintained after the holocaust of our enslavement were, for the most part, abandoned. The segregated Black communities contained the remnants of African culture. It provided single mothers and everyone else protection, and support. Our rush to move out of these segregated communities in pursuit of the individualized and illusive American dream that has turned into as Malcolm X said, "an American nightmare."

Both Black males and females experience this nightmare equally: White supremacy is not a respecter of gender. Yet its effects are easily detectable in the lives of Black boys and men as we are at the bottom of most quality of life indicators.

For example, Black males currently have the highest dropout rates, the lowest scores on standardized achievement tests, the worst attendance records, the highest suspension and expulsion rates, and the lowest graduation and GED completion rates. Less than eight percent of Black men have graduated from college compared to seventeen percent of whites and three percent of Asians.[5] Black males have the highest incarceration rates, the highest unemployment rates, and lowest life expectancy. Black men die at a rate that is at least 1.5 times the rate of young white and Latino/Chicano men, and almost three times the rate of Asian men. As the death rate drops for men ages twenty-five to twenty-nine for most groups, it continues to rise among African men in America. In our case, more deaths are caused by homicide than any other cause. The percentage of Black men in prison is close to three times that of Latino/Chicano and nearly seven times that of white men. While Black men represent fourteen percent of the population of young men in the U.S., we are almost fifty percent of the prison population. If the current level of incarceration continues, an African male in the U.S. would have about a one in three chance of going to prison during his lifetime.

We cannot overstate this enough, the horrendous conditions facing far too many Black males is not unintentional. The system is merely doing what it is designed to do: destroy all things African.[6] Therefore Black mothers must parent from this perspective and reality.

Figure 1

The Possibilities of Manhood Development Involving
Mothers (women) and Fathers (men)

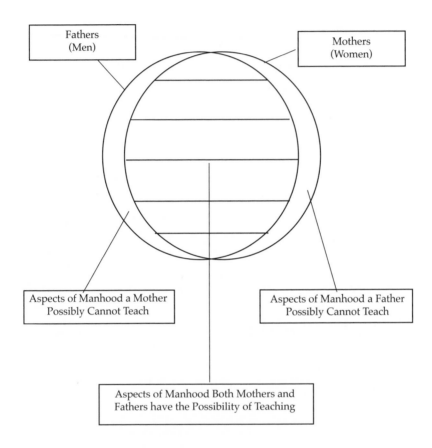

Figure 2

The Possibilities of Manhood Development Involving
Mothers, Fathers, and the Community

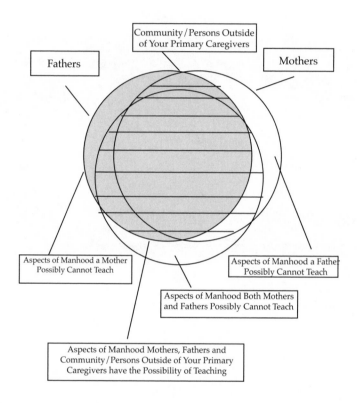

Figures 1 and 2 originally appeared in Bush, L. (1998). Manhood,
masculinity, and Black men: Toward an understanding of how
Black mothers raise their sons to become men. Claremont
Graduate School. Claremont, CA.

Key Points for "Beyond the Debate"

1. Mothers/women do not relinquish or excuse yourselves of the responsibility of raising your sons because you have been mislead to believe that raising a boy is a man's job.

2. Because of the amount of time Black women spend with boys you are the most significant factor in the development of Black boys.

3. Mothers can raise their sons to be strong and successful men; yet, we all, both men (fathers) and women (mothers) need help.

4. Mothers raise your sons with the understanding that are a significant number of external forces against them.

Chapter II

The Historical Legacy of Black Motherhood

For Africa to me... is more than a glamorous fact. It is a historical truth. No man can know where he is going unless he knows exactly where he has been and exactly how he arrived at his present place.

—Maya Angelou

Despite the challenges that statistics concerning Black males provide, we hold our destiny in our own hands; and these are largely the hands of Black women—one of the most powerful forces on the face of the planet. Therefore, it is important for Black women to realize that the responsibility of raising their sons is a task that has always been central to the development of Black communities, societies, states, and empires.

Historically, African civilizations viewed this relationship as so sacred that it was distinguished as the key kinship bond for the anchoring and stabilizing of Black societies. You may ask why single out the mother-son relationship? Are not other kinship bonds such as father-son or mother-daughter equally important? The answer to the latter question is yes. Those relational ties are also essential to the healthy functioning of Black communities. We are highlighting the mother-son relationship because the mother-son relationship has historically been prioritized as the foundation of many African societies. We will illustrate through an examination of the founding of two African empires that the mother-son relationship served as the basis by which the independence and sovereignty of the society was established and defended. There are historical models in African culture of Black mother and son relationships that esteem single Black motherhood as crucial to the development of Black boys and Black societies.

Ancient Egypt and Nubia as well as the Medieval West African Empire of Mali all privileged the mother-son relationship as the foundational kinship bond for the establishment of their sovereign states. In fact if it were not for the Black woman in all three of these African Empires, each of these societies would not have been founded nor would they've survived during periods of social turmoil and chaos. We may ask what the relevance of ancient and medieval African societies is for contemporary Black women raising their sons in the twenty-first century. The answer to that question can be found in raising another question, why did these African societies view motherhood (this includes single motherhood) as the most important family role for the building of their nations? Put another way, without the strength, determination, courage, and wisdom of Black mothers there can be no vital, thriving Black communities.

In ancient Egypt and Nubia the quintessential queen mother and Black woman was Auset, also called Isis by the ancient Greeks. Her hieroglyphic symbol was a throne because she was considered the foundation of her nation and people. It was through her that all kings were legitimized and therefore the sovereignty of the state. In other words the Black woman was considered the essence of authority, freedom, and independence in African societies. In the great national epic of ancient Egypt often referred to as the story of *Ausar and Auset*, Auset is the central character and in many respects the most important. Although she is a queen her life is not easy and full of difficulties, trials, and tribulations. Her brother-in-law Set out of spite and jealousy murders her husband and king Ausar. She is dispossessed of her home, land, property, and country and forced to live as a widow. Her brother-in-law illegally takes over her kingdom, annuls her authority and banishes her from her throne. Although her husband is murdered she is still able to conceive a child with him through her magical abilities.

After giving birth to her son Heru, Auset is left alone to raise her child and prepare him for kingship. Auset is a single Black female with the sole responsibility of raising her fatherless son. This task is not easy for her, and she often is on the run because her brother-in-law has placed a bounty on her head for fear that her infant son will grow up to reclaim his rightful place in the kingdom. Sometimes Auset and her son have to live in the most dangerous places in order to hide from Set. Auset all alone protects her son from the "scorpions" and evils of life to ensure that he reaches manhood and fulfills his destiny as leader and king. Ultimately due to the wisdom, devotion, and leadership of Auset, her son does reach manhood to reclaim the throne from Set and reestablish justice and prosperity in the land. Indeed as a child, Heru experienced great misfortune before realizing his destiny as God-King. He lived without a father and his mother was always under great stress due to being chased by her brother-in-law Set. Heru was able to escape the many pitfalls and snares of life because his mother was there to protect and guide him—it was his mother Auset who raised him and prepared him for manhood and leadership. This story is a remarkable and beautiful example of how single-Black motherhood was viewed as the heart of ancient Egyptian and Nubian culture. Nile Valley civilizations represented the first states and empires in human history, so it is telling that these African societies portrayed Black motherhood as indispensable to the development of the state and national culture. The esteem for women and motherhood continued throughout the history of Nile Valley civilization. The Kushite King Taharqa of Egypt's 25th Dynasty left a long inscription praising his mother and Nubia's queen-mothers, called the Kandake, ruled as sovereign monarchs and even led their nations into battle.

The Medieval West African Empire of Mali also portrayed Black motherhood as the foundation of this great civilization. The legendary epic of Mali's founding king *Sundiata* described Sundiata's mother Sogolon Kedjou as a wise and devout mother who raised her son for manhood and kingship after being ridiculed and exiled from her family and homeland. In the *Epic of Sundiata* it is prophesied that Sogolon will give birth to a great and mighty king who will make Mali great. The problem, however, is that Sogolon is described as a very ugly and hideous woman with an unattractive hump on her back. It was not expected that such an unsightly woman could be the bearer of greatness. Her ugliness and hump was not only an indicator of her physical appearance, but also symbolic of the pain, anguish, and burdens that she had experienced in life. The ancient storytellers of Mali were communicating that the most humble and lowliest of people can produce excellence.

Once Sogolon gives birth to Sundiata her problems are magnified. The boy does not appear to be a prince and in fact he is the source of great embarrassment and disappointment. He is an ugly child with big eyes and a big head and to make matters worse; he crawls until he is seven years old. Sundiata represents the classic underachiever who is also developmentally delayed in both his physical growth and social skills. Sogolon and her son Sundiata become the objects of derision and are laughed at by their family and community. Sogolon becomes so overwhelmed with despair by her son's underdevelopment that she begins to abuse him and scold her child by saying, "Oh son of misfortune, will you never walk." She blames her son for all of her problems and even suggests that God is punishing her by giving her a "problem child." Amazingly Sundiata responds to his mother's frustration and pain by consoling her and deciding at that point he will walk. From that moment on Sundiata begins to mature into a fine boy and ultimately a young man.

We have not discussed Sundiata's father King Nare Maghan for the simple reason of our wanting to emphasize the story of Sogolon. Sundiata's father dies while he is still a child and therefore like the Heru child in ancient Egypt, Sundiata is raised for kingship by his mother. Likewise Sogolon and her son are banished from their family and kingdom by jealous family members, and subsequently they roam homeless seeking refuge in many neighboring countries. They are accompanied by Sundiata's younger brother and sister as well as a griot that was appointed to Sundiata by his father. Therefore, Sogolon spends the rest of her life as a single-Black woman with the responsibility of raising three children. Sundiata's griot serves as his teacher and mentor as well a counselor and confidant for his mother Sogolon. Despite the unfortunate circumstances Sundiata was properly reared and educated for manhood and kingship. In fact the story tells us that, "between his mother and his griot, the child got to know all that needed to be known." Ultimately Sundiata does become king and reclaims the throne of Mali after years of exile and wandering with his mother. So, as for the question, "can Black mothers raise our sons?" the historic civilizations of the Nile Valley and West Africa respond with a resounding yes!

The stories of Auset and Sogolon epitomize the struggles and triumph of Black motherhood. Both women experienced abandonment, exile, loss, death, pain, despair, and anguish. Both women had the primary responsibility of raising Black boys and preparing them for manhood and kingship. Both women transformed their hardships into victory and thereby helped to propel their communities and nations forward. They are both models of who Black women have been and who they can become in our present and future.

Heru and Sundiata represent the struggle of many Black boys growing into manhood and leadership. Their mothers raised both boys because their fathers died while they were still small children. The two boys both experienced great misfortune in their lives and were often the object of ridicule and systematic assault. Much like Black boys today Heru and Sundiata were "sons of misfortune." Black male children and adults present the most dismal figures in all the categories of health, education, life expectancy, employment, and wealth development. Black males are disproportionately represented in the child welfare system, juvenile justice system, and the criminal justice system. Black males report the lowest figures for college attendance and graduation and the highest figures for homicide. Yet like Heru and Sundiata because of the diligence of their mothers, Black boys still have the power to turn misfortune into majesty, disappointment into destiny, and grief into greatness—this is the way of the GodKing.

The life and experiences of Ben Carson, a Black male neurosurgeon and the Director of Pediatric Neurosurgery and Medical Institutions at John Hopkins University, exemplify the persistent, triumphant spirit of Heru and Sundiata. Ben Carson was raised by his mother, a single Black female who he describes as the most important factor in his life achievements. In his book, *Gifted Hands*, Dr. Carson explains how he went from being a supposed dumb fifth-grader to a world-class neurosurgeon through the guidance and encouragement of his mother. His mother did not place limits upon Ben and his brother or restrict their minds because they were living in the inner city of Detroit where drugs, gangs, violence, unemployment and poverty were commonplace. Neither did she allow the reality of racism nor white supremacy to diminish or discourage her sons' potential to be excellent. Ms. Sonya Carson required that her boys only watch two to three television programs per week and devote the rest of their time to reading books. She advocated for her boys at school, set high expectations, and praised them when they did well. Like Auset and Sogolon, Ms. Carson was preparing her son for leadership and greatness. Certainly all Black mothers are called to do no less than what these women did for their sons and that is believe in them and set the highest standards of success and achievement.

We hope that you will be open to allowing us to help restore and guide you in your prominent and powerful role of raising our boys into strong, powerful, successful, and conscious warrior men.

Key Points for
"The Historical Legacy of Black Motherhood"

1. Black women have raised powerful sons under adverse conditions throughout history

2. Ancient Egypt, Nubia, the Medieval West African Empire of Mali, and many other locations throughout Africa, all privileged the mother-son relationship as the foundational kinship bond for the establishment of their sovereign states

Chapter III

Early Development
Establishing the Sacred Relationship

A Personal Story

Recently, we (the authors) heard rumors about an eleven year-old boy who could really play this horn but we could never seem to catch his performance. He had quite a reputation in the local area gained from playing at various social events. Finally, we would get our chance to hear him at an education conference. His mother, Mrs. Davis, gave a proud yet humble introduction of her son then he strolled out looking unassuming as could be in a nice suit. He put that horn to his mouth and began to play us some Coltrane. He played that horn! Miles, named after the great trumpet player, got a standing ovation.

Idealistically, pregnancy should be a planned event between two married people who have been nurtured by an affirming community. Idealistically, the couple has attained a certain level of spiritual development, discipline, respect and maturity to handle the responsibilities of family-hood. Though we are not always aligned in such a model structure, the Creator still gives us at least nine months to prepare for the birth of a child. No matter what the circumstances were surrounding the child being conceived, each mother was divinely chosen as a vehicle to be a carrier and mother of a divine seed.

Divine seeds must be housed in sacred places; you must regard your womb in this light. You are more than just physically connected to your fetus. He is completely dependent on you for everything. Be careful who you let enter your internal space—literally—if anyone at all as some would suggest, during the time you are with child. You must also be protective of your external environment as well.

Long before your fetus develops ears, which become structurally complete at twenty-four weeks, your son hears, feels, and responds to you in different ways.[1] Without getting too abstract and technical, all matter in the universe vibrates and therefore is capable of giving, receiving, and responding to vibration frequencies. The food you eat, music you listen to, places you go, people you hang around, and even your thoughts vibrate and affect your child while it looks like no more than a tiny dot in your womb.

We also know that at around seven to eight weeks of gestation, the embryo develops its first sensitivity to touch. At about thirty-two weeks he is sensitive to heat, cold, and pain. The nose develops as early as eleven weeks and scientists now believe that fetuses can smell. Though a fetus's ears are not fully in place until twenty-four weeks, as early as eighteen weeks the inner ear and the brain have developed enough for your unborn son to hear sounds such as your heartbeat, blood moving in your umbilical cord, and loud noises. By twenty-seven weeks he can hear and recognize your voice and the father's voice or the voice of people that you are around a lot or even the voice of someone on a TV show that you may watch often.

To this end, we are saying that you must begin raising your son properly soon after he is conceived. His development depends directly on your nutritional, social, emotional, and spiritual state and development. Start taking care of him by taking care of yourself.

We are not nutritionists; please see your doctor concerning this matter. However, do remember what we said about food having vibrations so we will suggest that you eat as many "live" or uncooked fruits and vegetables as possible. Likewise try to stay away from processed foods. Also along these lines, be conscious of where you are eating, with whom you are eating, and who prepares your food.

Be aware of your emotional state. Studies show that an unborn child's heart rate, birth weight, and brain development are affected by the mother's emotional state.[2] You may need to cut some folks out of your life if you find that they make you angry or sad very often. Do things that make you happy and relaxed daily. Surround yourself with positive male and female energy.

Pray. Pray for yourself. Pray for his proper development in your womb. Thank God for choosing you. Thank your ancestors—their blood literally runs through his veins. It is not too early to pray for his protection, his friends, his teachers, his mate, and his purpose and destiny.

Read to him and speak words of power to him. Listen to some Coltrane, or a CD of African drumming and rhythms, or better yet buy an African drum and have it played for him regularly.

At some time before your son is born, write out your parenting philosophy and plan. If the father is involved, have him write these out separately. When you complete the exercise you will first share what you have written with one another. You may be surprised at the differences but it is better to work on getting on the same page now rather than during the heat of parenting. After you have reached consensus, share your list with your extended family network.

The writing exercise should start with a general statement about your approach to parenting, your overall goals, and your method of achieving what you hope to accomplish (see Section One contained in the Workbook). Do not be afraid to deal with issues that seem to be far away like dating or the circumstances he would be allowed to continue living in your home after he turns eighteen.

Another important task to engage in prior to birth is the selection of an appropriate name for your son. Words are indeed powerful as they carry the means to create thus the name will invoke certain energy every time it is spoken. Just think about the number of times over a lifetime one's name is called.

Choose a name like you are choosing it for eternity rather than as if it were the flavor of the month. The name should call him to a high purpose, should remind him of his destiny and potential, and remind everyone including himself of his divine nature. The name could also be significant and important to the family history.

Do your research to find a good name and its proper meaning. There are naming books such as *The Book of African*

Names by Molefi Asante. Also, the Internet can be very helpful in finding names, their meaning, and origins. However, it would also be wise to crosscheck what you find on the Internet with other websites and perhaps people in different parts of the world you have chosen the name from to ensure the authenticity of what you have found.

You do not have to settle on a name by the day of his birth. We suggest that you narrow the list down to three or four. After the child is born, spend at least a day with him, as you look to him to help guide you on the final selection. Do not waste time choosing a meaningful and powerful name for your son if you are going to end up giving him a nickname like "Stinky," "Booboo," or "Dookie." We know you mean it out of love; however, there are better ways to show your love and affection.

Within a few months after his birth have a baby dedication and/or naming ceremony. This ritual practice goes back thousands of years and has specific spiritual and practical implications: it is not a perfunctory event! The ceremonial ritual is an announcement and a call to action for both the visible and invisible worlds bringing them on one accord. Malidoma Somé in his book entitled *Ritual: Power, Healing, and Community* explains, "a ritual performed by a community liberates a certain energy that makes it possible for other rites to happen at a family and individualistic level."

A baby dedication, which is a ritual, is typically held in a church and conducted by the minister. The church baby dedication ritual is sufficient for your son. However, for those who may want to have and additional service or add to the church dedication below are some *basic* components.

Whenever possible rituals, such as naming ceremonies, are handled by people who have been trained as traditional African priests. If one is not available, choose a respected elder in the family or community, a minister, or another respected family member or friend. The venue is typically in your home, that of a family member's, or a community center. The place where the event is going to be held needs to be purified prior to the event. This can be done with prayers, the burning of sage or incense (frankincense) and/or a basic cleaning of the area.

Provide seating as much as possible in a circular format: The elders should have the most prominent seating. Just like in church, typically the baby is dressed or wrapped in the finest of white cloth.

The leader of the ritual begins the ceremony with a prayer called a libation. The objective of libation is to invoke and usher in God, other spirits such as angels, and ancestors. He or she may pour water on to the floor, in a bowl, or into a plant as an offering as he calls them and prays. Songs and dance may follow. A blessing/anointing/washing happens next typically by water, "blessed oil," white powder or other herbs or liquids depending on the tradition of the presiding priest or minister. Guests are invited to share offerings of well wishes, money, or other gifts. Offer a closing prayer where you thank those for coming, those seen and unseen, and wish them a safe journey home. A meal is always provided.

Key points for "Early Development"

1. No matter what the circumstances were surrounding the child being conceived, each mother was divinely chosen as a vehicle to be a carrier and mother of a divine seed.

2. Write out your parenting philosophy and plan and share with your extended family.

3. Pray for his protection, his friends, his teachers, his mate, and his purpose and destiny while he is in your womb.

4. Choose a name that calls him to a high purpose and reminds him and everyone else of his destiny, potential, and his divine nature.

5. Have a baby dedication and/or naming ceremony.

Chapter IV

Early Childhood
Setting the Tone

A Personal Story

"I have one son in prison and another in college. I had Marcus and Vincent fifteen years apart… can you believe that? I made many mistakes with my first son. I was younger when I had Marcus and I still like to party some. I tried to be his friend, buy him stuff, and was pretty easy on him when he was a child. I didn't make him listen to me. When he got in a little trouble in school for this and that I sort of thought 'boys will be boys' … and he is still a boy. In and out of prison and I am raising his son. But with Vincent, shoot, I didn't play. You got to let them boys know from day one that 'mommas don't play that.' I don't mean to be harsh but hey you have to have a plan. Yes a plan and stick to it." [from an interview with Mrs. Vickers, a fifty-seven-year-old married mother of two boys and who is raising her teenage grandson]

ges one to four are critical to your son's development.[1] Some social scientists suggest that an individual's personality is set by age five.[2] Whether this is an absolute truth is difficult to say. Yet, we contend that whatever pattern of behavior, good and bad, which is established during this period, will be difficult to change down the road. You must get your son's attention. Some behaviors that you think are cute now will hurt you later if you do not firmly deal with them. We will address some of these behaviors in this chapter, but first it is important that you understand genius within your son.

It is important to impart to your son that he is not a single, lone individual that must face life without the benefit of communal and ancestral wisdom. Often during our male rites-of-passage program we ask the young participants how old they are. Most of the responses range from the ages of twelve and seventeen years old. We immediately tell our male journeyers to add 100, 500, 1000, 5000, or even 1 million years to their age because they are actually a part of ancient human and African legacy that extends to the beginning of civilization. This ancient cosmic and ancestral legacy represents the genius that lies dormant within your son—brilliance that he must be told that he possesses so that he may claim and fulfill his destiny. The Black physicist Neil DeGrasse Tyson reminds us that we are literally and physically "relatives" and "kin" of our solar system, star dust, and the chemical elements that serve as the building blocks of life itself. Your son must come to realize that the genius he observes in nature and creation is the same genius that resides within him. Your son is a cosmic specimen, an offspring of the elegant, divine intelligence that governs the universe. This fact alone serves as the basis of his genius.

The genius of Black boys also resides in their ancestral memory and historic cultural legacy. Africa lies at the center of human history and the foundation of civilization. It is important for Black boys to know the significance of what it means to be a male of African descent. Teaching African world history to your son reawakens his memory and situates him firmly in the achievements and contributions of African peoples to humanity.[3] Your son will come to know that he is a descendant of the originators of language, mathematics, agriculture, astronomy, architecture, engineering, medicine, music, theology and science. Black boys must study how their ancestors in the Nile Valley civilizations of Nubia and Egypt founded the first nation states in history. Such knowledge informs him that he is capable of self-governance and leadership today. He must be aware that African priests taught Greeks philosophy and Romans imperial administration. It should be common sense to the Black boy that Africa birthed and cradled Judaism, Christianity, and Islam and gave the world its first concept of God (Supreme Being). The Black boy should aspire to be a master of business, commerce and trade because his ancestors in Ghana, Mali, and Songhay controlled international markets in West Africa that stretched from the Atlantic Coast to India in

Asia. The architectural genius that produced Great Zimbabawe and the Mosque of Jenne in Mali will inspire him to design and construct magnificent monuments and buildings today.

Even through the Middle Passage (Maafa), holocaust of enslavement, Jim Crow, white supremacy, racism and discrimination, Black boys should know the genius of the African freedom struggle in America.[4] Black boys should know despite the obstacles placed before African Americans they designed the city of Washington D. C. in the person of Benjamin Bannaker and invented the traffic light through the efforts of Garrett Morgan. He should know that Black men such as David Walker, Richard Allen, Martin Delaney, Frederick Douglas, and Bishop Henry McNeal Turner fought to defend the humanity of Black people against oppression and injustice. Equally important the Black boy should venerate his ancestral grandmothers like Harriet Tubman, Sojourner Truth, Maria Stewart, and Jarena Lee who pressed for women's equality and the dignity of Black women and men. The Black boy should be reminded that it was the genius of Black culture that produced the greatest men of the 20th century in the United States, Malcolm X and Dr. Martin Luther King Jr. These two men forced America to honor its own principles of freedom, justice and equality for all people. When your Black boy is bopping his head to the latest hip-hop cut he should pay homage to Duke Ellington, B.B. King, John Coltrane and Jimmy Hendricks. In other words it is genius that permeates and surrounds your son—he only needs to awaken to it, acknowledge its presence and devote his life to unleashing his own genius.

The word education is from the Latin word *educere* meaning to bring out; to bring out what is already there. This notion of education was already in existence in Africa and was stolen by Europeans.

Thus, your son, with respect to his learning aptitude, is only limited by your expectations. Challenge your son academically. At a minimum (he can do more!) your son should know how to read, add, and subtract before entering kindergarten (implied in this goal is the assumption that your son has already mastered recognizing his numbers, counting, shapes, colors, and the alphabet and their sounds).

You should view everyday activities as learning opportunities. Taking a bath, driving in the car, and going to the store provide excellent chances for you to go over numbers, do mental math, sing learning songs, and to point out letters, words, and shapes. Make it fun and be creative. Limit television and computer time to instructional programming and activities.

Tell him he is a genius. If you must give him a nickname, call him genius or "G" for short. The world's first "O.G."— Original Genius. Even when he does not appear to act like it and even when you do not believe it, by you saying it you will condition both his and your mind into accepting this proven fact. Do not stop here, also tell him that he is brilliant, that math is in his blood, and that science is as natural to him as his breath. Wake him up in the morning with these names and whisper them in his ear before he goes to bed.

While all the above attributes we are saying about your son are true, his ability to manifest and grow them depends on your ability to provide consistency and discipline. Mothers you must be a disciplinarian whether or not the father or any other man is involved in his life. In this next section we will address some common questions and issues that arise concerning discipline and other socially questionable behaviors.

Should your son fear you?

Any emotion or feeling that is out of balance is potentially harmful. However, we do recommend that you create what we are calling a "healthy fear" within him. You do not want a son that fears nothing nor do you want a son that fears everything. Thus a certain amount of fear is healthy. If your son fears you so much that he is barley able to hold his head high, look you in the eyes, and speak to you this is unhealthy; conversely, if he fears saying the wrong thing in the wrong way or tone around or to you directly, that is healthy fear.

As we said earlier, some things that you think are cute now, will not be so funny later. We have seen boys at this age tell their mothers to "be quiet" or "shut up" and we have also seen boys ages one to four hit their mothers. Sadly, in far too many instances the mothers have laughed or ignored the behavior. If he is allowed to act in this manner towards you now, he will think that these behaviors are okay at age sixteen. You must deal with these occurrences swiftly and firmly!

Should you spank your son?

For old-school parents the immediate answer to this question is, "YES!" Yet, there has been a significant and growing movement against spanking as a sizeable number of psychologists contend that it is not ever appropriate to strike your child. Spanking your son, if at all, needs to take place in the context of love, stability, consistency, tenderness, and communication. Without these it may do more harm than good. Ultimately spanking cannot be your only method of disciplining. The day will come when no matter how hard you hit him it will be of little if any consequence. He needs to be more fearful of your disappointment in him than of any type of physical punishment you can render.   If you decide to spank, please check the national and state laws in your region as spanking children of certain ages or at any age at all is now illegal in some parts of the world.

Should you encourage your son to cry?

Yes. One of the reasons men have a shorter lifespan than women is because we do not know how to utilize one of natures gifts. Crying releases, among other things, stress. But as we said earlier, any emotion that is out of balance is not good. We draw a distinction between crying and being a crybaby. We also need to distinguish between crying and whining. It is somewhat natural for your son to want to whine after age 1, and it is at this time, though he will probably continue doing it for the next couple of years, that you should begin making your displeasure of it known. Eliminating whining is part of the process of teaching your son how to speak clearly and with confidence and power. To eliminate whining, first you must have zero tolerance for the behavior. Second, set clear rules and definitions of the unwanted behavior. Third, demonstrate and practice an appropriate tone of voice. Fourth, set clear consequences for continued whining. Five, praise your son when he uses an appropriate tone. Last, be consistent in exercising all of the above.

Should you allow your son to grow long hair or to have an earring (or earrings)?

We acknowledge that what men and women do in this society is socially constructed and contextual. Moreover, our concept of what is abnormal is based on white middle-class expectations. There is nothing inherently wrong with a boy having long hair or an earring. Nevertheless as the parent you must consider a couple of factors: (1) we have noticed that boys, mainly due to how society responds to them, become so preoccupied with their hair and being "cute" that it actually begins to change their behavior—the last thing boys of this age need to be overly concerned about is their hair and "getting it done" and (2) an earring in boys' ears still carries with it two opposing stigmas— being soft or a thug; neither of which are positive. (There is a difference between having a soft side and being soft. In the way we mean it here, neither boys nor girls should be soft.). Though not necessarily true, both stereotypes are too much for a child this age to deal with given all the other challenges he will face from just being African and male in this country.

Given that clothes carry meaning, it is important that mothers implicitly discuss and show appropriate clothing for certain settings. This can be first done by only buying your son what you think is appropriate for him to wear. You can also point out appropriately dressed men to him wherever you go. More subtly, you can pay a complement towards someone who is wearing something that you would want your son to wear. For example, say: "I really like what he is wearing. He looks so handsome." You can say this directly to him, or to a third party while making sure he can still hear you.

Should you allow your son to play sports?

Organized sports activities for boys generally start about age four. Sports can be a wonderful way to teach your son about discipline, hard work, teamwork, competing, and the like. It can also be way to expose your son to additional positive male role models. However, playing sports has to be considered a privilege secondary to excellent grades and behavior. Nevertheless, excellence should be demanded from you in every area of you son's life including athletics. You do not need to know much about sports to demand that your son understands the difference between "giving up" and "giving out." A boy should never find a soft shoulder from his mother when he has decided to quit or give up on anything; rather, mothers must be clear that it is absolutely unacceptable. Mothers tell your sons in your own stern words, "I ain't raising no quitters!"

With that said, many of our boys have more balls than they have books. Athletics always need to be seen as a means to an end. In other words, athletics should be discussed as a way to go to college to get a free education. If your son is one of the fortunate few to become a pro athlete, most do not play their respective sport for more than three years. Even if he has a full career as a pro athlete, most will be unable to play past thirty-five years of age. Thus, how your son is going to use athletics to achieve what he wants in life should be a constant focus of discussions around sports activities.

Should I allow my son to be a pro athlete?

Boys around age five begin to talk about what they want to be when they grow up and many will already say that they want to be a pro athlete. Their choice simply reflects the behavior and focus of adults in their lives. We have enough Black pro athletes. We need more scientists and business owners. As your son talks about being a pro basketball player you ask him: "What kind of basketball player are you going to be? Are you going to be the kind that uses his money and fame to build Black schools and to own Black businesses?"

The above line of questioning is recommended no matter what career aspirations your son is expressing. You must help him find the "what," that is, what he wants to be, and perhaps more importantly, you must also help him develop the "who," that is, his character and the kind of person he is going to be in the profession he chooses.

You have to consciously stretch your son's horizons and possibilities. When you are reading a book, ask him what his book will be about when he writes it. When you drive past a construction site, tell him that one day he is going to own trucks and land and have people building buildings for him. When you see a president of a country, ask him how he would run a nation.

Just as becoming a parent should not be a haphazard event; hopefully it is becoming clearer that parenting Black boys takes a calculated plan of action. To help you in this regard, we have created the Manhood Development Progress Indicator (MDPI). Starting at age five, then again at ages nine, twelve, and fifteen you should conduct the indicator. The MDPI is a list of different areas in the lives of boys and men, such as Spirituality, African History and Culture, Love, Survival/Protection, and more (See Section Three of the Workbook for the "MDPI" work sheet by age).

Under each area or heading ask yourself (and your son as he gets older) the following: Is, who, how (that is, the method being used), what, where, and how often. For example, under the heading Spirituality ask: Is spirituality being taught? Who is teaching him about spirituality? How is it being taught? What is being taught? Where it is being taught? How often is it being taught? Your aim is to find holes, inconstancies, and imbalances. Holes occur where you find that no one is teaching a particular aspect of manhood, inconstancies are occurrences where you find that an aspect of manhood is not being taught enough or your son is receiving conflicting or incorrect information, and imbalances are where you discover that an aspect of manhood is only being taught by one gender or in one setting.

Key Points for "Early Childhood"

1. Some behaviors that you think are cute now will hurt you later if you do not firmly deal with them.
2. Your son's learning aptitude is only limited by your expectations.
3. Tell your son daily that he is a genius to build his self-concept.
4. Your son should have a "healthy fear" of you.
5. If you spank your child as a form of discipline, it needs to take place in the context of love, stability, consistency, tenderness, and communication.
6. Allow your son to cry but prevent him from becoming a crybaby or whiner.
7. Emphasize books over balls.

Chapter V

Boyhood
Starting His Educational Journey

A Personal Story

We met with Aretha, a twenty-seven year-old stay-at-home single mother, her son Xavier, his elementary school principal and his teacher, Ms. Wrangler. The school officials wanted to retain Xavier in kindergarten largely based on his behavior. They assured us that his academics were fine and that retaining him was the best solution. In fact, they insisted that he have the same teacher. Ms. Wrangler, a middle age white woman, who appeared to be kind and harmless, kept repeating how cute and adorable Xavier was, and that she "just wished she could take him home" [we will discuss the harmful effects of viewing Black boys in this manner in the next chapter]. *Against the recommendation of the school officials Aretha sided with us and Xavier was not retained. Though much of Xavier's behavioral issues appeared to be a matter of maturity, we worked with Aretha on being more consistent with her disciplinary practices. Xavier went to the first grade and had a very good year. This year, he is in the second grade, and will finish near the top of his class without having any significant disciplinary infractions. Since Xavier's experience with Ms. Wrangler, she has tried to retain four other students, all of whom are Black boys.*

As educators, scholars, researchers, activists, and parents we are extremely aware of the challenges awaiting Black boys in schools. We have already provided you with some general statistics and unfortunately there are many more that we could list. We could also present a host of educational and psychological theories that attempt to explain the lack of educational success that a significant number of

Black boys experience. But we need not look any further than what Dr. Carter G. Woodson,[1] Marcus Garvey,[2] and Dr. W.E.B. DuBois[3] told us nearly a century ago. Each of them wrote that the educational system in the U.S. was designed to uplift whites and maintain the illusion of their supremacy and to create in us the desire to protect with our lives their interests, wealth, land, and ideas.

Despite the aforementioned calculated purpose of the educational system, some Africans, building on their (our) long tradition of education and institution building, have created within, under, and on top of the white system of schooling.[4]

Black educational institutions and spaces provided us with the schooling we needed to achieve unbelievable results and success in the face of remarkable challenges. Thus, Black mothers should approach school with both the knowledge of the malicious function of the educational system outlined by Woodson, Garvey, and DuBois and the confidence that comes with knowing that African peoples have never been without a strong record of educational excellence.

School Environment

Earlier, we stated that the underlying design and purpose of American schooling is a sorting system, designed to sustain authority and control held by the white power elite,[5] and as such, have a limited capacity to develop schools of achievement for Black students. Student achievement data speak volumes about the ineffectiveness of public schools, as Black male students, by all measures, are academically less successful than any other racial sub-group. Popular hip-hop artist Ice Cube conceptualizes much of this sentiment when he said in a popular song: *"Ya'll want to know the crime of the century? A ghetto elementary. A mental penitentiary."* Given the reality that most Africans in American children will attend public schools, parents must leverage this system failing so many Black youth.

Thus, critical questions emerge, such as: What can parents minimally expect and demand from Black boys, their teachers, and the schools they attend? How does the Black community leverage a system to our benefit, that is, by all measures, ineffective at educating African American boys? What strategies should parents employ to ensure that Black boys reap the benefits of a much-needed education in order to compete in a capitalistic society, while still developing a positive self-concept? The answers to these critical questions lies in our understanding of the public educational system, our assumptions about the system as it relates to Black boys, and finally, how we engage the system—from how we prepare Black boys to how we interact with school personnel on their behalf.

Research on the topic of Black underachievement in public education has revealed alarming statistics concerning the educational lives of Black boys. A brief discussion of some of the data is necessary to gain greater insight and understanding into the mainstream schooling process, and its persistent reproduction of academic underachievement, criminal delinquency, and negative self-concept so pervasive among Black youth. An examination of the extent to which schools are failing Black boys gives context in developing "assumptions" about the schooling process for Black males, and the appropriate actions parents must take in engaging Black boys at home in preparation for school and at the schools they attend if we are to save them from these harsh realities. These are:

- Black males at all educational levels are more likely to be, (a) labeled deviant and negatively described by teachers, (b) have their abilities be inaccurately assessed by teachers, (c) receive nonverbal criticism from teachers, and (d) be disciplined and referred to the office.
- Recent National Assessment of Educational Progress (NAEP) scores in reading and math show that on average in the fourth grade, Black students are two years behind white students, and that by the eighth grade Blacks are approximately three years behind whites.
- In most major cities, Black males have disproportionate and dramatically higher suspension, expulsion, and grade retention rates.

- Risk factors for school failure increase exponentially when the Black, male gender, and low socioeconomic status intersect.
- There are more Black men in prisons and jails in the United States (about 1.1 million) than there are Black men incarcerated in the rest of the world combined.
- Black students are more likely to have unprepared, unskilled, less-experienced teachers.[6]

Considering these data, African American parents must change the approach to schooling for Black boys, adopting fundamental assumptions about schools and personnel serving Black males. Knowing what you are up against as a parent is critical in developing an approach to the schooling process for Black males. The approach must incorporate strategies that, (1) seek to lessen the negative impact on the future of Black males by creating school environments that are less hostile to Black males, and (2) that teach Black males about the unwritten rules in mainstream society, as well as coping strategies which allow Black males to navigate successfully in school in order to reap the benefits of a good education despite the barriers that the school poses.

Assumption #1: In general, school personnel believe that academic underachievement among Black students can mostly be attributed to failing Black communities and families, citing poor, uneducated, and uncaring parents as causal factors.

In short, many teachers believe they are good teachers, despite the overwhelming underachievement of Black students in their own classes and in the school. Teachers often attribute positive student results to good teaching, but conversely, poor student results are often attributed to factors outside of the control of the teacher, dismissing the relationship between poor teaching and racist school environments on student achievement. The strong relationship between teacher expertise and instructional practice, and student learning has long been documented. Divorcing teacher practice from student achievement is a practice popularly accepted in schools and, despite overwhelming research linking teacher practice and student achievement, remains largely unchallenged. This practice ignores the impact of teacher expertise, personal outlook (bias, stereotype, and misconceptions), and interpersonal interaction between teachers and Black males on Black male student achievement. Additionally, abdicating professional responsibility for learning, or lack thereof, ignores research on effective teaching practice for Black students, as well many examples of successful teachers and schools serving Black students.

How does the dynamic of teachers removing themselves from the equation in student learning play out in the classroom? The answer: Apathy and no accountability for Black boys. Apathy and lack of accountability for the achievement of Black male learning by teachers has resulted in schools that consistently marginalize, under-educate, under-prepare, foster poor self-concept, and create adversarial relationships with Black students and their families that ultimately contribute to alarming social statistics and depressed academic achievement among Black males. It is not uncommon to hear racial slurs, negative stereotypes, or insensitive characterizations of Black students and their parents in the professional and personal discourse among teachers and other school staff.

Negative perceptions concerning Black males and their families create the context for the persistent reproduction of Black male underachievement and fuel a normative school culture that relieves teachers of any personal investment in student learning among Black males,[7] nullifies the need for further professional development or self-reflection due to the fact that teachers do not view themselves as part of the problem, and creates hostile classroom and school environments for Black males. The result: a school environment in which Black males are disproportionately referred out of class, suspended from school, and achieve at low levels. The institutional response, if there is one, is flawed as well, because, again, most personnel attribute poor achievement to failing families and communities, and improvement strategies rarely hold teachers accountable for improved practice, but instead, focuses on "fixing" the students.

Professional development on effective instructional practices for Black males often falls on deaf ears, as teachers do not see themselves as part of the problem, nor the solution. As educational consultants and school administrators we have facilitated and attended numerous presentations focusing on the analysis of student achievement data and effective instructional strategies for teachers. We often find that teachers, even when shown gross achievement gaps among students in their own classes, dismiss, marginalize, or become apathetic about the data. Corresponding strategies for improving teaching practice as it relates to Black children are confronted by teachers unwilling to reflect on their own practice and its relationship to both positive and negative impacts on underachievement among Black children. Many teachers dismiss professional development or simply refuse to teach in schools with a high enrollment of impoverished children of color, causing high teacher turnover in urban schools. Ron Edmonds, educator and author, describes best the psychological strongholds held by teachers that prevent them from doing what's best for students:

> How many effective schools would you have to see to be persuaded of the educability of poor children? If your answer is more than one, then I submit that you have reasons of your own for preferring to believe that basic pupil performance derives from family background instead of school response to family background...we can, whenever and wherever we choose, successfully teach all children whose schooling is of interest to us.

Assumption #2: In general, school personnel have low expectations about the intellectual abilities of Black boys.

Low expectations for Black achievement in the classroom are the contemporary manifestation of a long established legacy of the institutional degradation and oppression of African people by Europeans. Since the times of our enslavement, Africans in this country have combated white supremacy. Racist ideologies of white superiority and Black inferiority have been systemically propagated by all facets of society, and handed down from generation to generation. White supremacy has taken many forms, but the basic premise has remained the same: the oppression of African people. Blacks in this country have endured the brutality of the slave trade and the institution of slavery; have been described as three-fifths of a human in the Constitution of the United States; braved racist segregationist laws, such as the Grandfather Clause which outlawed basic freedoms if your father was a slave, and Jim Crow laws which created statutes to limit social and economic advancement; fought terrorists groups such as the Ku Klux Klan and police authorities seeking to keep Blacks living in fear; and fought injustice in education, civil rights, health care, the legal system, housing, and other areas for basic civil liberties.

Contemporary forms of white supremacy have continued in the form of unfair hiring practices; unequal health care; biased legal and judiciary systems; substandard housing that lack basic infrastructure such as community centers, schools,[8] banks, grocery stores, job opportunities, health care facilities, availability of drugs and weapons, and disproportionately higher numbers of liquor and small convenience stores and gun shops; dilapidated, substandard schools employing a disproportionately higher percentage of inexperienced, incompetent teachers than in affluent areas; and law enforcement that profiles, criminalizes, and brutalizes Black males.

Music and the media have played an influential role in the continued degradation of the African persona. Positive portrayals of Black people are rare in the news and media. Television, movies, and music videos portray Black people as gangstas, drug dealers, drug addicts, pimps, thugs, dummies, athletes, comics, buffoons, entertainers, strippers, hustlers, uneducated, illiterate, prisoners, thieves, rapist, murderers, sex-crazed, and the list goes on. Not that those things don't exist in some Black communities, or any community for that matter—but the social ills in the Black community are sensationalized and exaggerated far beyond perspective. Nightly news segments report disproportionately higher criminal acts of Black males. The constant stream of negative portrayals and images of "dangerous" Black males, coupled with the typical European-centered education that most people in American public schools receive, creates a near certainty of developing low expectations from teachers about Black male students.

The majority of teachers, that is about eighty percent, in U.S. are white, middle class women who have been socialized in such a manner to fear, mistrust, and misunderstand Black boys, negatively impacting interpersonal relationships between Black boys and their teachers.[9] Negative perceptions of Africans in general, but Black males in particular, lead to instructional decisions, such as placement in gifted or honors classes, placement in rigorous coursework, and classroom interaction, that are predicated on low expectations.

The classroom experience for Black boys, therefore, is wrought with verbal and non-verbal criticism that marginalizes student strengths and exacerbate student deficiencies; frequent office referrals for escalating classroom disruption, most often attributed to an eroding and increasingly adversarial teacher/student relationship; frequent suspension from school as school administrators find it easier to discipline the student rather than confront a teachers' bias and poor instructional delivery; and removal from grade-level courses and placement in low-level, remedial classes, often full of peers experiencing similar difficulties, and taught by incompetent, inexperienced teachers. On the opposite end of the spectrum, high achieving Black students are often treated as an enigma by teachers, having to constantly prove their abilities and work twice as hard as their white peers to achieve at high levels. These students suffer as well, as they are pressured to adopt a sense of "racelessness," having to disassociate themselves from the African persona and peer group to achieve at high levels.[10]

Assumption #3: School curriculum omits the African contribution to human progress, modern civilization, and transformational advancements in science, technology, math, government, literature, art, and religion.

What are the characteristics of a Black male high school graduate having gone through an *optimum* public school experience? When operating at its best, students graduating from a public school system have earned high marks in college preparatory coursework and are qualified to successfully complete post-secondary education. Although there is a significant gap in college-going rates between white and Black students, there are Black male students fitting the aforementioned profiles throughout the country. Much can be celebrated about these students, as they have achieved at high levels, often in spite of the public schools they attended. What remains problematic about traditional public education is that Black students, whether they excel or not, will graduate from the public school system, having gained little knowledge about themselves, their culture, and their heritage.

We view this as problematic. Traditional, European-centered school curriculum contains very little information regarding people of African descent. The topics and people that are covered—typically the slave trade and slavery, and the Civil Rights era, are mentioned as side-notes to the primary events under study, lacking both an African-centered perspective, depth of exploration, and meaningful analysis. All students, not just African Americans, experience a great disservice, as the enormous contributions of African people to the world are treated in school curriculum as trivial, token, and African people are treated as bystanders, victims, and pawns in European and American history.

As such, an education that engenders negative attitudes toward people of African descent is not only inadequate, but also detrimental and contradictory in preparing Black boys to fully participate in a global society as equal participants. Traditional, European-centered education creates an incredible delusion of the African self-concept, creating the unique challenge for Black boys of redefining themselves in a positive light, while simultaneously fighting a society that holds Black people in poor regard and striving to interact successfully within the same society. Black boys must receive an education that includes the enormous contributions of African peoples to civilization and human progress, to develop a positive self-concept to fully participate as world citizens.

Effective School Engagement Strategies

Developing Early Literacy and a Life-Long Joy of Reading in the Home

Developing school readiness in the areas of literacy, mathematics, and study skills is vitally important for Black boys given the persistent and ineffective school environment presented to many of them. Early literacy and reading fluency are the foundation of school success. Research suggests that students who leave first grade without the ability to fluently read grade-appropriate materials develop ever-widening deficits in learning as they matriculate through school. Fostering a joy of reading requires the explicit, purposeful development of a home environment and culture that deeply values reading. Reading should be a daily occurrence. Frequent reading builds reading fluency, comprehension, problem-solving skills, vocabulary, articulation, and writing. Additionally, reading proficiency is essential for success in other subjects, which rely heavily on textual comprehension such as math, science, and social studies. Below are some strategies to help foster a life-long joy of reading:

- Posters, rugs, and toys displaying the alphabet, numerals, shapes, and colors should be placed throughout the house and should be taught and reinforced by parents and siblings frequently to build early literacy development in youth from zero to six years of age.
- A children's "library" should be created and housed in focal living area to show the importance of literature and books. The actual books should mostly contain books featuring African characters, cultural traditions, and experiences.
- Reading to, with, and independently—From an early age, Black boys need adults and siblings reading to and with them every night.
- As Black boys become older and enter school, consistent quiet time in the home must be

established for reading. A one-to two-hour block of quiet time in the home is important to establish sacred reading, studying, and homework time. This time should be uninterrupted by the television, radio, or phone. After a few weeks of implementation, all children in the house will begin to establish a routine.

- Throughout their entire educational career, Black boys should have personal reading assignments prescribed by parents to supplement the required school reading. Frequent trips to the bookstore or library can be used to select books outside of school, and should focus on personal interest, biography, history, African experiences, etc. Starting at about fourth grade through high school, Black boys should be reading one personal, age-appropriate book per month, in addition to the reading assigned at school. Parents should model this behavior by reading during the quiet time as well.

- Parents should monitor school reading with frequent discussions with their sons, as well as daily homework completion checks. It is important to remember, that there is no such thing as, "I don't have any homework." Organizing, rewriting, refining, and reviewing notes from the school day are important activities to reinforce the concepts taught at school.

Developing After School and Vacation Routines

After school hours are vitally important to school success. Juvenile delinquency and crime occurs most often just after school, when many youth are unsupervised and have few positive activities to engage their time. Additionally, with many parents working during and after school hours and often well into the evening, coupled with a steady decline of positive recreational facilities and activities in urban communities, parents must take explicit control of how their sons are using their after school and vacation time.

A definitive, well-monitored after school routine, whether parents are home to supervise or not, is the first building blocks to fostering accountability, responsibility, work ethic, and school success within Black males. Parents should begin with establishing a time to be home, that allows brief time (30 min.) to interact with teachers if needed, and get home. Unsupervised children should check-in with parents by phone. Students should then begin the after school routine, which involves relaxation time and eating, chores (we will say more about chores in this chapter), homework, and study.

Parent/Teacher Conferences, School Complaints, Basic School Structure for Support

The challenge for parents is to counteract the negative per-ceptions of school staff about your son. This does not necessarily mean that the relationship between the parent and the school has to be negative. In fact, it is quite the opposite. The goal for parents is to demonstrate an active role in the educational lives of your sons; make explicit your desire to develop a healthy supportive relationship between yourself and the teacher; and leverage the relationship to increase the educational yields for your son by influencing school personnel to regard your son with as much care, concern, and expectations, as you do. Parents will find that developing good relationships with school insiders will increase the opportunities afforded your son, as well as to force school personnel to challenge their personal beliefs about Black boys, one personal relationship at a time.

Creating Positive Relationships with School Insiders

Building a network of school insiders to advocate for the best interest of your son is not only provides additional support for Black boys, but also adds an additional layer of accountability for your son. Interviews of high achieving Black students growing up in urban communities identified both family and school personnel as important in helping them to meet their personal potential. Parents should take every opportunity to familiarize themselves with the significant adults within the school. As educators often serving as insiders, we have experienced numerous examples of adults stepping in before a student makes a poor decision; teachers intervening with other teachers on behalf of students; counselors providing access to accelerated programs or opportunities to students who do not fit the "traditional mold," secretaries ensuring that paperwork is completed so as not to disrupt vital programs that students need. Finding allies and advocates, such as teachers, counselors, custodians, instructional aides, and administrators for Black boys in the school, is critical to developing a network of "insiders" to watch over your son. Black boys often lack the "social capital," or insider access provided by school insiders, that is required to overcome school bureaucracy, racist, exclusionary, or elitist selection criteria, which bars the participation of Black boys. The parent's role in creating building your son's social capital at school cannot be stressed enough. Some strategies:

- Back to School night attendance is vital to help counteract negative notions and stereotypes that your sons' teachers may hold of Black boys. These nights should be used to introduce yourself along with your son to each of his teachers, school administrators, and counselors, ensuring each that you are looking forward to a productive year, are confident that the school will provide excellent educational environment for your son, and that your son is held to the highest of academic and behavioral standards at home, and you are eager to partner with the school in bringing out the fullest potential in your son.
- Be a parent volunteer. In this capacity you are able to do such things attend fieldtrips and assist the teacher in the classroom which send a strong

message to the school insiders and to your son as well.

Developing a "Network of Achieving Peers"

As school administrators, we spent a considerable amount of time responding to discipline complaints from teachers about students. When these complaints led to conferences with students and their parents, we often found that parents were surprised about the company that their child kept, and believed that the influence of other children was the primary culprit in their child's poor behavior. We often used this opportunity to begin a dialogue with parents about peer groups, telling them that other parents describe their child in the same manner. Children tend to associate themselves with friends that are like them. Parents should employ the following strategies to both improve your son's peer group, and to monitor and guide their experiences together:

- Familiarize yourself with your child's friends, and their parents, by requiring that your son introduce each of his close friends.
- Create structured opportunities for your son and his friends to spend time in and around your house to familiarize yourself with the type of friends your son is choosing.
- Require your child and his friends to devote time to their studies as a precursor to leisure time. Studies have shown that Black students, compared to other racial groups, spend the least amount of time studying together.
- Engage your son and his friends in frequent discussions about school, and appropriate behavior in and out of school, to teach good decision-making.
- Do not hesitate to bar fraternization with other students who are consistently exhibiting

different behavior than what you desire for your son.

Goal setting, Priorities, Rewards, and Consequences

Setting academic and personal goals is a good way to begin the year. This should start by asking your son to write down the goals he has for himself based on his personal and academic strengths and weaknesses. He should also develop long-term goals as well. Ask your son to tell you:

- What was my poorest subject? Why did I perform poorly in this subject or class? What have I learned about myself (strengths and weaknesses) this past year? What will I do differently?
- Describe a significant personal or academic accomplishment from this past year? What did I learn about myself? What did I do to be successful in this area? What will it take to experience continued success in this area?
- My parents are most proud of what about me?

Monitoring Student Progress

A commonly used weapon against Black families by the school is lack of communication, failure to respond to school literature. Progress reports, report cards, school communications, and test scores must be monitored carefully. To help you in this endeavor in Section Five of the Workbook you will find the "College Preparation Worksheet by Grade" and sheets to help you monitor your son courses towards college and the grades he earns.

Improving Motivation & Encouraging Scholarship, Excellence, and Responsibility

Along with the demands of school by at least age five chores should be a regular part of your son's routine (See Workbook "List of Suggested Chores by Age"). The ability to sustain hard work that may not be considered entertaining or fun is a skill that does not get enough attention and focus. Starting with cleaning up behind himself progressing then to taking out the trash and yard work to caring for his younger siblings or grandparent are meaningful and useful assignments. Beyond hard work you are trying to teach your son this ancient African principle written in the *Teachings of Ptahhotep: The Oldest Book in the World,* which says, "The good son is a gift of God and exceeds what is told of him." In other words, the good son does extra.

The out of school activities or training also need to include a rites of passage. Rites of Passage is the vehicle or mechanism used to instill the cultural memory and consciousness of a people by way of ritual as it marks the seasons, transitions, or changes in the self. Birth, initiation, marriage, and death are generally the most celebrated transitions. In Chapter II we outlined the importance of the baby dedication ceremony as the first rites-of-passage celebration. Continuing along that same vein, the next set of rites of passages we suggest also carries with it the same purpose of gathering the community, your son, and the invisible world to be on one accord but with the specific focus of creating a man. Men—African men—are not created by accident.

At age eight have a ceremony that celebrates the life of the child and that also serves as a notice to him and the community that a transition is on horizon and we, the community and child, must collectively and purposefully prepare the way. Your son must leave the ceremony with an understanding that being part of a community carries responsibilities. Your son is also given a list of expectations required for his rite of passage at age twelve (See Workbook, "Rites of Passage Guidelines, Age 12). The second ceremony involves testing the child and celebrating his successful passage. A portion of the test will be given the day of the ceremony while others will be documented in a portfolio maintained by your son and you and his father. Lastly, the adolescent should leave this ceremony with a list of expectations for the next rite of passage that is to occur at age eighteen or before he leaves for college (See Workbook, "Rites of Passage Guidelines, Age 18). During the last celebration the adolescent will be tested and present a portfolio that was maintained by him.

Key Points for "Boyhood"

1. The educational system in the U.S. was designed to uplift whites and maintain the illusion of their supremacy and to create in us the desire to protect with our lives their interests, wealth, land, and ideas.

2. Develop early literacy and a life-long joy of reading in the home.

3. Develop a network of achieving peers.

4. Develop after school and vacation routines.

5. Create a rites-of-passage program in your home.

Chapter VI

Adolescence
The Psycho-Social Sexual Development

A Personal Story

"I can remember this like it was yesterday. It was hard but I had to do it. He was 16 and had been asking me a lot of questions. We had talked some about it before through the years so I guess that is why he felt he could come to me. So we climbed up on my bed—it was too funny but he listened. I had a pickle and a condom and I showed him how to put it on. I was nervous but I did it—somebody had to. As I thought about it, I said, 'who better to teach him about sex than a woman?'" [from an interview with Ms. Black, a forty-six year-old single mother of two boys]

Under the best of circumstances, the adolescent years will be, at least in some ways, challenging. Part of the challenge is purely a function of natural development. Driven by impulses, your son will struggle at times to think through the consequences of his actions. This is coupled with a growing physique, increased strength, and expanding intellect that will all conspire to trick him into believing that he is invincible. He is going test your authority. Be prepared for the test.

This is the time when many Black mothers will be tempted to excuse themselves from the raising of their sons believing that he has to have a man to deal with him concerning the developmental issues he is experiencing. Surely we recommend you have men involved; however, you cannot abandon your son now. He needs you more than ever. There is so much more that your son can learn from you during this time. Thus do not fall into the trap of thinking your son needs or even wants you to be his friend. You are his mother, not his friend. One of the many characteristics of being a mother is the ability to be friendly when the situation calls for it but this is a long distance from being his friend. For example, friends will buy their sons whatever clothes they want and allow them to wear them in any manner they desire. Mothers, being aware of how Black men are viewed in society, provide their sons with the clothing that gives their sons the best opportunity for them to be successful at school and to make it home safely.

Speaking of how society views your son, it is important to understand that he has been adultified since early elementary school. This is why we find that Black boys are punished more frequently and more severely than their classmates who commit similar or the same offences.[1] Black boys are not given the benefit of the sentiment that suggests, "boys will be boys" when they misbehave. Rather their misbehavior is seen a calculated adult choice therefore being worthy of severe punishment.

The early adultification of Black boys has ramifications for the main topic of this chapter, sex. Young Black males dwell in a sexually charged environment more so than other males because they are adultified and because of the stereotypical images of Black males as the Mandingo—a character having a super-sized penis and a supper-size sexual appetite to match.[2] He is the forbidden fruit, which makes him more tempting to others, which is a lot for a young adolescent male to deal with. Helping him to understand and deal with this is your responsibility as his mother.

Also as your son begins to look, sound, and act like an adult it is sometimes tempting for a Black mother to assign to their son, who is still a boy, the role of "the man in their life," and/or "the man of the house." This is dangerous ground. He cannot handle the responsibility and power that comes with the position. Thus making your son the man in your life will only backfire as he will treat you as a peer rather than his mother making it particularly hard for you to set rules and limits.

With that said, mothers can and they must teach their sons about sexually related issues. There is some evidence that suggests that when mothers do teach their sons about sex that they have been better at communicating it than many men in that they have included issues beyond "protect yourself." These mothers deal with such issues as romance, responsibility, "being ready," and the feelings of the girl.[3] When we think about it, what individual would better to teach about all the aspects of sex, other than a woman, in this case a boy from his mother?

"I am waiting until I get married," was a common response given by girls when we were coming up, when asked about having sex. It was respected, expected and hoped for, especially among fathers with regards to their daughters. What about our boys? Have we conceded to a societal double standard about sex? Do we have the same hope and expectation for our sons? What age is appropriate to even have the discussion? How do we successfully counter the messages and images of pop culture, which honors and glorifies sex without commitment, sex without emotion, sex without love, and sex just for sexin'?

Every marketing medium uses women to sell and promote their product. Our music and movies reduce our women to pulsating, gyrating genitals completely void of feeling and self-respect. Black men are portrayed as emotionless, callous, calculating pimps whose primary goal in life is to "get cash, ass, make a baby...and dash." Where then do our boys receive ethical instruction, direction and guidance that would in fact provide them with the proper context for developing healthy, mutually beneficial relationships? Are we guilty of perpetuating these and other reckless notions in our daily lives? Mothers must understand that their personal relationships with men serve as instruction for there sons. In essence, sons first learn how to treat women by watching the way women in my life are treated.

The task is not an easy one, but mothers raising boys alone, must assume the traditional roles and responsibility of fathers. That means that you are going to have to develop the courage and boldness to explain nocturnal emissions (wet dreams), erections and base desires. If you find yourself unable to discuss any of these topics, you must seek assistance from a man that you respect and believe will instruct your son in accordance to our highest values. That is to say, you need the help of a brother with a moral vocabulary.

When is it appropriate to allow your son to date or have

a girlfriend? This conversation is crucial given the expectations that accompany the idea. Much like hitting and talking back at age three or four, we think it is cute when our children first say, "I got a girlfriend or I got a boyfriend." It is relatively innocent in kindergarten and usually based on who colors the best, or has the prettiest bow on her head. That is not the case during pubescent years. Please be aware that today's youth are engaging in increasingly risky behavior as early as fifth grade. "Friends with benefits" is commonplace with middle school aged youth. This is the practice of girls performing sex acts on boys without any ties. You have to ensure that your son does not become a participant in or a victim of this activity. We say victim because of the number of outbreaks of chlamydia and other STD's that have occurred recently in middle schools across the country. We do not abdicate the responsibility of teaching our children about dating and sex to the schools or other organizations that teach pregnancy prevention and related issues like STD's. We instead insist upon being the primary provider of such instruction.

The rule is: you cannot have a girlfriend until you are in your senior year of high school, and you must be on the Honor Roll. In addition, you must demonstrate to *my* satisfaction, the preliminary qualities of manhood, i.e., responsibility, respect, conscious of and committed to community development, purposed and spiritually grounded just to name a few. This rule maybe viewed as being unreasonable, or better yet, unlikely. However, setting this rule as a standard is absolutely necessary.

Rationale: We say senior year because it is difficult enough for our Black boys to be successful in school as it is, they do not need any other distractions. If you do not have Honor Roll status, it is clear that you need more time to study. How can you have time for a relationship, but not enough time to study? By twelfth grade, and between seventeen and eighteen years old, given that they have met the above criteria, a relationship is then permitted. By this time, they will have completed requirements for Rites of Passage in that they should have a firm understanding of self and their place in community. The relationship is monitored; and this becomes the opportunity for you to observe your son to see if he practices the values instilled in him. He must not be left alone to deal with the emotions and expectations of a relationship. You have to be there to pick up the pieces of a broken heart. At this age, it is only a question of when, not if. Failing to do so will force him to internalize his feelings, and mature without developing adequate tools that help maintain a healthy self-concept, as well as maintaining a healthy respect for women.

An open and honest dialogue about sex should be ongoing and age appropriate. The discussion about nocturnal emissions at age eleven is not the same discussion at age fourteen. It is our recommendation that you lead with discussing the importance of abstinence. Contrary to popular belief, everybody is not *doing it*. This does not mitigate the need and necessity to teach contraception, but you must have a standard. He must be taught that it is okay to wait until he is married as a matter of fact; it is the preference. Simultaneously, you or someone you trust must be able to teach methods of contraception. The most common method used by teenagers of course is "withdrawal." It is the most common, because without proper instruction, he will find himself in predicaments where it is the only method available to him. This comes from lack of planning, and lack of discipline. Do not let your boy grow with the belief that it is the girl's responsibility alone to prevent pregnancy. He must understand that it is as much his responsibility if not more, as it is hers, to prevent unwanted pregnancy. Explain to him that condoms not only prevent pregnancy, but they protect from sexually transmitted disease. Share with him statistics that show how prevalent disease is among his age group. Do not forget to tell him that he can contract sexually transmitted diseases from oral sex.

Teen pregnancy in Black communities is probably the single greatest cause of dreams deferred. The cycle of single parenting is perpetuated because we have not done all that we can to address the causes. Sex has become more recreational and perhaps even, a panacea for the pain and hurt caused by society. That is to say, when all else fails around me, sex feels good and I am in control of this one small part of my life. This is done without consideration of consequence. Thus when the girl becomes pregnant, the first question asked is usually, "How do you know that it is mine?" This is particularly painful to the girl involved, as she believed him when he said, "I love you and you are the only one for me, and if you do get pregnant, I will be there for you."

Consequently, another child is brought into the world, into our community without the benefit of two parents; another Black girl is saddled with the responsibility of raising a child alone; another Black boy has successfully used his game "to get some" and reduce the Black girl to nothing more than a sperm receptacle. And, to compound this felony, some mothers have aided and abetted their sons in this cowardly, selfish and reprehensible act by not insisting and demanding that responsibility be taken. Instead, teach your son that if he brings a life into this world, his life changes effective immediately. He will instantly take on the role of provider and care giver. College, sports and any other plans now take a back seat to his primary responsibility of raising a child.

Teach him that he must be a self-mastered man. Challenge him to mold his character to that which emulates the best in Malcolm, Marcus and King. Implore him to honor the legacy, life and love of Betty Shabazz, Anna Julia Cooper and Coretta Scott King. Teach him that to honor, love and respect women, is to honor love and respect you.

Key Points for "Adolescence"

1. Making your son the man in your life will only backfire as he will treat you as a peer rather than his mother and make it particularly hard for you to set rules and limits.

2. Mothers can and they must teach their sons about sexually related issues.

3. Sons first learn how to treat women by watching the way women in his life are treated.

4. The rule is: your son cannot have a girlfriend until he is in his senior year of high school, and he must be on the Honor Roll.

5. Talk to him about condoms and how to use them.

6. Talk to him about sexually transmitted diseases. Do not forget to tell him that he can contract sexually transmitted diseases from oral sex.

7. Teach your son that if he brings a life into this world, his life changes effective immediately: He will instantly take on the role of provider and care-giver.

Chapter VII

Young Adulthood
Transitioning to College

A Personal Story

"I have two boys and two girls and all four graduated from college. You never really stop being a mother, your approach might change but you never really stop being a mother. Some folk think, 'If I get them through high school then I am done.' Now why would you invest all that time in them and then just be done? You may have to let go some; but that is a long way from being done! ...I remember when my youngest boy was in college and a letter came to our house from the university; something told me to open it. The letter said that he was on academic probation. I thought and thought and I prayed too about what to do. I didn't call him—you got to let them be a man sometimes; but I had to do something. I called his big brother, who was also away at school and told him to talk to him. I don't think I even told his daddy... his daddy might have killed him. Hmm... I guess it all worked out. He and his brother got their Ph.D.s now." [from an interview with Mrs. Carter, a sixty year-old woman, who is married with four children]

As we begin this chapter, we want remind you (or inform you) that when your son reaches young adulthood your work as a parent is not over. As a matter of fact, in many respects a new aspect of parenting is just beginning. The support that you have for your son at this point in his life should be as strong and as vigilant as when he first entered kindergarten.

Do you remember his first day of school? Do you recall the uncertainty that he had? Can picture walking him on the school grounds more than likely holding him by the hand? Can you think back to what must have been running through his mind? If he was like most, he was thinking something like this; would I be accepted, how would I take care of myself, am I going to miss being home and seeing my family, am I going to make friends, do I belong here?

On this first day how did you ensure him that everything was going to be okay? We have you thinking back to this time for a very good reason and that is for him and for you his first day of kindergarten is going to be much like him entering into college. While the physical stature of your son has changed and, yes, he is more emotionally and mentally mature, but going into this new environment called college is like his first day all over again and he is having those same questions that he had starting kindergarten. As a parent while maybe not holding his hand this time, you will still function as his source of support and comfort.

Thus far we have focused on the uncertainties your son will have as he enters college. However, we would be remised if we failed to take you through what that first day of kindergarten was like for you as a parent and how that relates to you at this time. While that day is fresh in your mind can you think back to the thoughts you had? Your questions may have been similar to this; is he ready for this, did I prepare him well enough, did I teach him everything he needs know to take of himself, will he remember and will he do all things that I taught him, will I miss him?

In the above paragraph we could have very easily substituted the word kindergarten for college and those same questions would be relevant to what thoughts and emotions you are going to have when he "goes off" to college. For some parents when they began to answer these questions, it becomes very difficult. In some cases the idea of their son going to college, particularly in the instances where the son is exploring the possibility of going away, the mother can consciously or unconsciously sabotage their son and their college aspirations. Sabotaging your son college plans can sound like an overstatement, but in fact this occurs often, particularly if the mother has grown depended on the son for emotional support. This can especially be an issue if you are single mother. In other cases mothers are literally fearful of their sons going to college believing that they will become different and that they will be exposed to ideas and people who may contradict the things they raised their son to believe. As a result, we have heard statements like this: "Son, maybe you should think about attending community college, and if you stay home it will be cheaper, if you leave who is going take care of the things you do around the house?" Or they subtly make known their disapproval and this effectively in many cases deters the son from going away from home for college.

Again we state, "your job as mother is never over." We want to make this blatantly clear because we know the idea exist among parents that once your child leaves the house then your job is done. We think a parent may rush to be done is for several reasons; one is simply the desire to be free of the burden and responsibilities of parenthood. Although, we know there is no such thing as ever really being free of this burden, but parents are often enamored with this notion. In the case of college we think it also has a lot to do with your own uncertainties as parents in terms of you believing that you cannot help him. We think that this may be especially true for mothers who did not attend college. This chapter will discuss how you can provide this support, not in terms of teaching you what it means to support your son, but to provide you with insight into what he will be facing in college so you can ask the right questions, navigate your way through his responses and give you a heads-up so to speak of the challenges college brings.

Before going further, we realize that not every child wants to go to college and that there are other pathways to success. That being said, your son should leave high school with the academic skills necessary to attend and be successful at a university. Your son deciding he does not want attend college is one thing; not having the skill set and academic background to attend, is another. Lastly, while our statement about there being other avenues to success outside of going to college may be true, it may also be misleading as well as Black college graduates on average earn about double of what Blacks make per year with just a high school diploma.

If your son chooses a career track rather than going

to college, he will still need a plan. He will still need some additional training and schooling. Thus, much of what we have to say to mothers of sons who are going to college applies to mothers who sons are learning a trade. Perhaps, however, these mothers need to be more vigilant and involved as the way to a career without college may be a little less structured or apparent. As early as possible begin to introduce your son to people who work in the area he is interested in pursuing. Encourage him to find a job if possible in his area of interest before leaving high school as vocational careers can be highly based on work experience (rather than educational background) and who you know.

Quitting Is Not An Option

For the first several weeks of school it is quite possible that your son is not going to like college. After the initial adrenaline rush of being away from home or not being in high school the reality of the demands of college will quickly set in. Usually during the first several weeks of college your child will call often and if possible visit often. This is okay as they are merely trying to adjust. At this point allow your son to initiate the contact with you. Calling or visiting your son a lot at this time would appear as you not having faith in him. If your son is having difficulty he may express to you that college is hard and that college is not like high school, he doesn't like the people or that he is homesick. You may not know it, but your son is testing you with these questions. He is testing you to see what your response will be. He his trying to see if at some point, if he chooses not to continue school or to come back home, would you be okay with that. So if your response is baby you don't like it maybe that is not the school for you, or honey you know if that school is too tough maybe you should just take some classes at the community college. While he may not immediately pack his bags to return home or drop out your response lets him know that he has a way out and that you will not be disappointed if he leaves. If you went to college or not all you need to know that college is not going to be easy and yes there are going obstacles that your son is going to find difficult. However, when your son talks with about this, what you do is listen and remind him that he is more than capable of meeting any challenge that come his way and that by no means is quitting an option. Letting him know that quitting is not alternative, sets the mindset he needs to endure the challenges he will face.

Must Have Conversations

The following items are important conversations at minimum that you should have with your son while he is in college. These topics are not meant to be one-time conversations but should be revisited often throughout his time in college. The following items are also what we call launch pad conversations in that they often can leap into further discussion of other important areas.

Encourage him to join the African student Alliance (BSU) or other organizations that will allow him to develop his consciousness, expose him to leadership opportunities, and learn valuable social skills.

Often we believe that college is all about the books and that is not necessarily the case. It would be foolish to emphasize social involvement over study time or class time. We often hear parents say that you are not going to school to do nothing else but study. The truth is that college presents opportunity for your son to grow academically and socially with a great deal of this learning occurring outside of the classroom. Studies clearly show that the more a student is engaged with his college by being involved in a college organization increases the likelihood of him not dropping out and being successful while he is there.

Know his friends.

Talk to your son and ask him questions regarding the type of people he is hanging around. You cannot assume that because now that he is college that everyone there is doing positive things. The same type of negative people that you fought to keep him away from in high school exists on the college campus ten-fold. Your son would be asked to hint a joint, to commit criminal acts, and at very least encouraged not to study and skip class. While these elements exist it is still critical to encourage him to establish friendships. Positive peer interaction is essential in his academic and social success. In the case of African American males, research shows that peer interaction is a determining factor of students staying and graduating from college. If your son connects to a positive peer group it will pressure him to perform to the group standards, keep him socially and culturally grounded particularly if your son is attending a predominately white institution.

Revisit with him the key points you learned in Chapter V (sexuality)

Understand that since your son is in college he is a Black man that is about something. Unfortunately, at this point in our history in the United States, because of the years of outright assault on Black men, many young brothers are exhibiting behavior that is contrary to the person they really are. Not only do you realize that your son is headed in the right direction others will recognize this fact, including many well and not-so-well intentioned young ladies. He looks like he will be a good baby daddy. Simply, he is more than likely going to have women vying for his attention, and how is handles this can dictate his course in life. Remind him to use protection. Ask him if he is looking for a meaningful relationship.

Inquire if the girls he deals with are in college or did he meet them elsewhere. Ask to talk to his girlfriend and invite her to visit if possible. College is a great opportunity for your son to meet his future wife. So to say leave those girls alone is not necessarily the best advice to give your son; you are asking him to lie to you if that is your expectation. A good college girlfriend who has a lot going for herself as well can be a powerful ally in the battle for him to graduate. What you want to mitigate, as a parent, is the distraction that dealing with women can have while you are in school.

Be understanding of the academic rigor of college.

When your son was in high school chances are he was not being fully challenged. This means that he was able to make it through without putting much time and energy into his studies. College is different in that in order to be successful he must focus his time and energy on his books. This is going to not only be an adjustment for him but for you too particularly for those sons who live at home and go to school. He may not be able to do all things he did before he started college such as, watching younger siblings. We are not saying that he should be free of any household responsibilities but his study time should be respected and by you allowing this to happen is one of the most supportive things you can do as a parent of a college student.

Do not be intimidated.

Do not be intimated by the paperwork or the terminology of the college institution. Processes like financial aid forms can be intimidating even to those who have filled them out before. Your son is going to need your financial information every year right around the months of January and February. If he is on financial aid then he going to need financial information from you. If these months pass and he has not asked you for this information call him immediately and find out what is going on. You may be a private person and may not like discussing your finances with your son and you don't want anybody in your business, you will have to just get over this.

College is different then high school in that they treat your son and his records as private information even if he is not yet eighteen. There is a federal law called the Family Educational Rights and Privacy Act (FERPA), which all you need to know about this is that the school no matter who you call or visit will not disclose anything about your son as it pertains to college without his consent. Therefore, the only source of information that you have about how well your son is doing is from him. Your son is bright and he not above using his brightness to deflect any inquiries into his academic performance if he not eager to share it. We know parents who demand to see their student's grades particularly for those parents who are contributing financially to their son's education. We found that by parents just asking about grades whether your son is forthright or not goes a long way to let him know that you sill expect excellence.

Talk about finances.

The phrase "a broke college student" is real and, in fact, it is a benefit. Going to college often means delaying employment and thereby postponing the possessing of material items, such as a car. Many young men desire to work for the sole reason of getting a car and we know young men who choose work over college just to get one. We suggest that you encourage your son to go as long as possible without car, particularly if it is his responsibility for the payments, gas and insurance. Once he buys a car, he is locked into having to work while he is in school and will no longer have the option of being a full-time student because of this financial obligation.

College is his full-time job and he and you should treat it as such. He should be encouraged not to work more than twenty hours a week and if it is financially possible he should not work at all in freshmen year. The first year of college is so critical that it is better for him to take out student loans then to work more than forty hours a week or to work at all in his first year. When he works he should seek to first try to find a job on campus. This will allow him to network with college personnel and also college work is limited to twenty hours a week and they will work around his school schedule.

In addition, discuss with him the importance of having

good credit. Your son is young and is difficult for him to comprehend consequences of decisions he will make today that will affect him five years from now. Credit card companies are like vultures on a college campus and they are willing to provide your son with as much credit as they can. The use of credit is something with which parents struggle. Can you imagine the temptation that credit will bring at the age of eighteen or nineteen? Since the credit card companies are willing to provide credit this is an excellent time for him to build a good credit history that will benefit him when he decides to purchase a car or a home. Many young people experience credit problems and what generally prevents them from purchasing a home is the credit problems that they experience while in college.

Key Points for "Young Adulthood"

1. Parenting continues while you son is in college.

2. Support your son while he is in college by expecting nothing less than graduation.

3. Create an environment conducive for study.

4. Talk to your son about his college experiences.

5. Become knowledgeable about the resources available to your son at the college.

Services On Campus You Should Know About:

- **Financial Aid Department**: Office that processes your son's student aid. Also provides assistance in filing your Free Application for Federal Student Aid (FAFSA).

- **Learning Center**: Department that offers among, other things, free tutoring.

- **Educational Opportunity Program (EOP)**: Program developed to aid college students from low-income families. Services include counseling, summer bridge programs, and grants.

- **Job Placement or Career Centers**: A department that connects students to on and off campus employers. Also provide assistance in interviewing skills and resume writing.

- **African Student Programs or Multicultural Center**: Cultural centers that provide support and programs geared towards the specific needs of African American students.

- **Ombudsman**: A position on some college campuses that serves as someone who is responsible for investigating and resolving complaints from students against the institution.

- **Health Center**: Provide heath services to students on campus. Health centers have medical and psychological doctors and nurses available for free on campus. Also is a place where free condoms are available for students.

Closing Words of Encouragement

Note that we did not directly define what a successful Black man is; though you have probably gathered from reading the book that we approach African manhood from a particular perspective. Nevertheless, one's definition of success is something that should be under regular review. And we must use discernment as we study and grow in consciousness and come under regular scrutiny because we are constantly bombarded with definitions that are counterproductive to African peoples. You should have an ongoing dialogue with your son concerning a joint vision of success. Your definition and vision for successful African manhood should be influenced by at least three factors: (a) our history and culture drawing on our ancient African experience as well as our experience in the Americas; (b) a collective family and community consensus; and (c) an awareness of current political and social circumstances.

For further Study

Drawing on our history, here is a list of Black men and women who your son should be familiar with beyond the purpose of the memorization of facts. Rather, you should use these men and these women to study their strengths and weaknesses, to articulate why they should be remembered, to compare and contrast them with each other and him, and to speculate and construct the historical figures' definition of successful manhood. Each of these names reminds you that there is much that boys can learn from both men and women. Learning more about them will teach young brothers how to serve our community as well as develop into strong, conscientious, and successful men.

King Narmer
Imhotep
Ahmed Baba
Gabriel Prosser
Denmark Vesey
David Walker
Henry McNeal Turner
Booker T. Washington
Charles R. Drew
Elijah Muhammad
Martin Luther King, Jr.
Kwame Nkrumah
Bobby Seale
Queen Hatshepsut
Harriet Tubman
Fannie Lou Hamer
George Washington Carver

King Piankhi
Sundiata
Toussaint L'Ouverture
Richard Allen
Nat Turner
Frederick Douglass
W.E.B. DuBois
Marcus Garvey
Carter G. Woodson
Paul Robeson
Malcolm X
Huey P. Newton
Queen Nzinga
Sojourner Truth
Ella Josephine Baker

A Final Lesson

We leave you with a brief story of Denmark Vesey as a shining example of African manhood.

Denmark Vesey was born in Africa or the Caribbean some time between 1767 and 1770. He was enslaved by a slave trader named Captain Joseph Vesey and traveled around the world. At age thirty, he bought his freedom and settled in Charleston, South Carolina where he opened a highly successful carpentry business becoming a fairly wealthy man for his time. People described him as a proud, tall, and straight man (meaning that he did not bend or hunch over when he dealt with folks) who taught his children that Blacks were in no way inferior to whites.

In 1821, inspired by Toussaint L'Ouverture and the Haitian Revolution, Denmark Vesey began to plan a rebellion. In fact Vesey, who could speak several languages, studied Toussaint's tactics to help him construct a blueprint for his attack. As many as 9,000 individuals were involved; and the date was set for the second Sunday in July 1822. However, the plan was revealed and he was eventually captured on June 22, 1822. He was sentenced to death and was hung on July 3 and he never told any part of his plan to authorities. The judge in his case said:

> It is difficult to imagine what infatuation could have prompted you to attempt an enterprise so wild and visionary. *You were a freeman; were comparatively wealthy; and enjoyed every comfort,* compatible with your situation. You had therefore much to risk and little to gain. From your age and experience you ought to have known that success was impracticable.

What we gather from Denmark Vesey's life among other profound characteristics and attributes is that, though he was a man with high social status, well-traveled, literate in multiple languages, economically advantaged, and "free," he had a definition of success beyond individual accomplishments. Apparently Denmark Vesey's definition of success and manhood was tied to the well being of the community. In other words Denmark Vesey must have said to himself: I am not successful; I am not free until we all are free. What kind of man would I be if I thought otherwise?

List of Suggested Readings

A Parent's Guide to Teenage Sexuality by Jay Gale

Beating the Odds: Raising Academically Successful African American Males by Freeman A. Hrabowski III, Kenneth I. Maton, and Geoffrey L. Greif

Black College Students Survival Guide by Jawanza Kunjufu

Black Men, Obsolete, Single, Dangerous?: The Afrikan American Family in Transition by Haki R. Madhubuti

The Book of African Names by Molefi Kete Asante

Boys into Men: Raising our African American Teenage Sons by Nancy Boyd-Franklin and A. J. Franklin

Can Black Mothers Raise Our Sons? by Lawson Bush V

Chains and Images of Psychological Slavery by Na'im Akbar

Coming of Age: African American Male Rites of Passage by Paul Hill Jr.

Countering the Conspiracy to Destroy Black Boys by Jawanza Kunjufu

Gifted Hands: The Ben Carson Story by Ben Carson and Cecil Murphey

The Mis-Education of the Negro by Carter G. Woodson

Ritual: Power, Healing, and Community by Malidoma Somé

SBA: The Reawakening of the African Mind by Asa G. Hilliard III

State of Emergency: We Must Save African American Males by
Jawanza Kunjufu

The Teachings of Ptahhotep: The Oldest Book in the World by Asa
G. Hilliard III, Larry Williams, and Nia Damali

Notes

Chapter I

1. See the following works to understand the dearth of research in this area: Bush, L. (2000). Solve for X: Black women + Black boys = X. *Journal of African American Men, 5*(2), 31-53; Bush, L. (2004). How Black mothers participate in the development of manhood and masculinity: What do we know about Black mothers and their sons? *Journal of Negro Education,* (73) 4, 381-391; and King, J., & Mitchell, C. (1990). *Black Mothers to Sons: Juxtaposing African-American Literature with Social Practice.* New York: Peter Lang.

2. Sudarkasa's work provides an early foundation for problematizing the experiences of Black single mothers: Sudarkasa, N. (1980). African and Afro-American family structure: A comparison. *Black Scholar, 11,* 37-60; Sudarkasa, N. (1988). Interpreting the African heritage in Afro-American family organization. In H. McAdoo (Ed.), *Black Families* (2nd ed.) (pp. 27-43). Newbury Park, CA: Sage Publications; and Sudarkasa, N. (1993). Female-headed households: Some neglectful dimensions. In H. McAdoo (Ed.), *Families Ethnicity: Strength in Diversity.* (pp. 81-89) Newbury Park, CA: Sage Publications.

3. For a background on how the breakdown of Black extended family networks has pejoratively impacted communities see: Wilson, M. (1986). The Black extended family: An analytical review. *Developmental Psychology, 22,* 246-258; Wilson, M. (Ed). (1995). *African American Family Life: Its Structural and Ecological Aspects.* San Francisco: Jossey-Bass; and Wilson, M., & Tolson, T. (1990). Family support in the Black community. *Journal of Clinical Child Psychology, 19,* 347-355.

4. Scholars rarely account for the age of the mother and almost never such factors as how long mothers have been a single parent and under what circumstances. See Barrett, A., & Turner, R. (2005). Family structure and mental health: The mediating effects of socioeconomic status, family process, and social stress. *Journal of Health and Social Behavior, 46,* 156–169;

Brody, G. H., Murry, V. M., Kim, S., & Brown, A. C. (2002). Longitudinal pathways to competence and psychological adjustment among African American children living in rural single-parent households. *Child Development, 73,* 1505–1516; Lipman, E. L., Boyle, M. H., Dooley, M. D., & Offord, D. R. (2002). Child well-being in single-mother families. *Journal of the American Academy of Child & Adolescent Psychiatry, 41,* 75–82; and Sterrett, E., Jones, D., & Kincaid, C. (2009). Psychosocial adjustment of low-income African American youth from single mother homes: The role of the youth–coparent relationship. *Journal of Clinical Child and Adolescent Psychology, 38,* 427-438.

5. For an account and breakdown of Black male statistics according to demographical, psychological and social (including health), political and economic, and educational issues see Collier, D. (2007). *Sally Can Skip But Jerome Can't Stomp: Perceptions, Practice, and School Punishment.* Joint Doctoral Program in Educational Administration, California State University, Los Angeles/University of California, Irvine.

6. Williams, C. (1987). *The Destruction of Black Civilization.* Chicago: Third Word Press.

Chapter III
1. For fetus developmental stages see Lightfoot, C., Cole, M. &, Cole, S. (2008). *The Development of Children (Sixth Edition).* New York: Worth Publishers.

2. Field, T., Diego, M., & Hernandez-Reif, M. (2006). Prenatal depression effects on the fetus and newborn: A review. *Infant Behavior & Development 29,* 445–455; Jablesky, A. V., Morgan, V., Zubrick, S. R., Bower, C., & Yellachich, L. A. (2005). Pregnancy, delivery, and neonatal complications in a population cohort of women with schizophrenia and major affective disorders. *American Journal of Psychiatry, 162,* 79–91; and Lou, H., Hansen, D., Nordentoft, M., Pryds, O., Jensen, F., Nim, J., & Hetnmingsen, R. (1994). Prenatal stressors of human life affect fetal brain development. *Developmental Medicine & Child Neurology, 36,* 826-832.

Chapter IV
    1. Lightfoot, C., Cole, M. &, Cole, S. (2008),
    2. Dennissen, J., Asendorpf, J., & van Aken, M. (2008). Childhood personality predicts long-term trajectories of shyness and aggressiveness in the context of demographic transitions in emerging adulthood. *Journal of Personality, 76,* 67-99.

    3. For readings on African history see ben-Jochanna, J. (1981). *Black Man of the Nile.* New York: Alkebu-lan Books; Diop, C. (1974). *African Origin of Civilization: Myth or Reality.* New York: Lawrence Hill and; Jackson, J. (1970). *Introduction to African Civilizations.* New Jersey: Citadel Press.

    4. The following two books will provide you with a good background with the impact of the maafa, our enslavement, and white supremacy: Akbar, N. (1984). *Chains and images of Psychological Slavery.* Jersey City, NJ: Mind Productions & Associates, Inc. and; *Cress* Welsing, F. (1991) *The Isis Papers: The Keys to the Colors.* Chicago: Third World Press.

Chapter V
    1. Woodson, C. (1977). *The Mis-Education of the Negro.* New York: AMS Press.

    2. DuBois, W.E.B. (1969). *The Souls of Black Folk.* New York: Fawcett World Library.

    3. Hill, R. (Ed.). (1987). *The Marcus Garvey and Universal Negro Improvement Association.* Berkeley: University of California Press.

    4. Bush, L., Bush, E., & Causey-Bush, T. (2006). The collective unconscious: New thoughts on the existence of independent Black institutions. *The Journal of Pan African Studies,1,* 48-66. Retrieve from http://www.jpanafrican.com/docs/vol1no6/TheCollectiveUnconscious_vol1no6.pdf.

    5. The following classic works support our notion about the purpose of schooling in the US: Bourdieu, P. (1986). The forms of capital. In J. G. Richards (Ed.), *Handbook of Theory and Research for the Sociology of Education* (pp. 241-258). New

York: Greenwood; and Bowles, S. & Gintis, H. (1976). *Schooling in Capitalist America: Education Reform and Contradictions of Economic Life*. New York: Basic Books.

6. see Collier, D. (2007)

7. Foster, H. L. (1995). Educators' and non-educators' perceptions of Black males: A survey. *Journal of African American Men, 1*, 37-70.

8. See the following article that outlines the prevalence of racism in schooling: Ladson-Billings, G., & Tate, W. (1995). Toward a critical race theory of education. Teachers College Record, 97(1), 47-68.

9. Kunjufu, J. (2002). *Black Students. Middle Class Teachers.* Chicago: African American Images.

10. See Fordham, S. & Ogbu, J. (1986). African-American students' school success: Coping with the "burden of 'acting white.'" *Urban Review, 18*, 176-203 for an explanation of the acting white notion; however, read Perry, T., Steele, C., & Hilliard, A. (2003). *Young, Gifted, and Black: Promoting High Achievement Among African-American.* Boston: Beacon Press for a thorough challenge of Fordham and Ogbu.

Chapter VI
1. Ferguson, A. (2000). *Bad Boys: Public Schools in the Making of Black Masculinity.* Ann Arbor, MI: The University of Michigan Press.

2. Bush, L. (2005, August 11). Stopping the stereotypes. *Black Issues in Higher Education, 22*, 66.

3. Bush, L. (1999)

About the Authors

Lawson Bush, V, Ph.D./Nana Kweku Baakan is Professor and Director of the CSULA/UCI Joint Ed.D. Program in Urban Educational Leadership. In addition to his book, *Can Black Mothers Raise Our Sons?*, he has published over 25 articles addressing African American educational history, African-centered education, school desegregation, and Black male schooling and developmental issues. His aforementioned research foci situate him as the leading expert on the relationship between Black mothers and their sons and the development of Independent Black Institutions (IBIs) in the United States. His work in the academy has been augmented by his tenure as the founder and director of the following programs and organizations: Imani Saturday Academy, Neighborhood Manhood Development Program, and the Tehuti Educational Consortium. Lastly, he has been happily married for 15 years to his wife Tonia and is the father of three children: Chioma, Thandiwe, and Lawson/Heru the 6th.

Rev. Edward C. Bush, Ph.D., Vice President of Student Services for Riverside Community College has over 15 years of experience in higher education involving the recruitment, retention and educational success of African American student. He is a published author with articles appearing in: *Black Issues in Higher Education*, *Community College Week*, *Educational Horizons* and the *Community College Journal*. His research has focused on African American male achievement in California Community Colleges, and student leadership development. Dr. Bush is a founding member of the African American Male Education Network and Development (A.M.E.N.D). He currently resides in San Bernardino where he enjoys spending time with his wife Jenise and children, Nia (17) and Khari (15).

Kennon Mitchell, Ph.D., is currently an Assistant Super-intendent of Student Services in San Bernadino, CA. He has served as principal, assistant principal, and teacher at both the elementary and secondary level. As principal, Dr. Mitchell developed and implemented the MAAT Academy, an African-centered after school intervention program targeting at-risk African American male students. The program served over 300 African American young men with great success for five years. Dr. Mitchell teaches part-time at the university levels, and research interests include, urban school renewal and African American school success.

A. Majadi, a native of Detroit and father of seven, currently serves as the President/CEO of the Boys & Girls Clubs of San Bernardino. He has more than 20 years experience in community program development, specifically gang prevention and intervention, and is a staunch advocate for education. Mr. Majadi is co-founder of the Inland Empire Black Community Coalition. He currently serves as President/CEO of the Black Contractors Association of the Inland Empire, President of the Black Contractors Association of California, is Founder and President of JADI Community Resource Development, Vice-President of The Westside Action Group, and board member for Regional Congregations Neighborhood Organizations as well as Transcendence Children & Family Services. A member of many committees and advisory boards, Mr. Majadi has made it his life's work to do all that he can to improve the quality of life and opportunity for Black people.

Salim Faraji, Ph.D. is Associate Professor of Africana Studies at California State University, Dominguez Hills. His research and scholarship represents the cutting edge of Africana Transdisciplinarity, transgressing the traditional boundaries of Religious Studies, African History, Nubian Studies, Ancient History, African Diaspora Studies, Martial Arts and Youth Development & Education. He is the author of the forthcoming book on Africa Word Press, *The Triumph of the Last Pharaoh: Roots of Nubian Christianity Uncovered;* and co-author of the book, *The Origin of the Word Amen: Ancient Knowledge the Bible Has Never Told* and a contributing author to the *Encyclopedia of African Religion* and the forthcoming reference work, *The Oxford Dictionary of African Biography*. He is a researcher and practitioner of African and African American martial arts and one of his prospective projects is to re-publish his work *MontuScholar: Mysticism and Martial Arts in Africa and the African Diaspora*. He also presents a ministerial background having completed his Master of Divinity at the Claremont School of Theology and formerly served in the United Methodist and African Methodist Episcopal Churches. He has been conducting rites of passage programs for over 18 years in a diversity of settings. He is currently a practicing African Traditional Priest and has been initiated in both Akan traditions of Ghana, West Africa and the Sacred Order of the Sons of Ra.